Most days, I feel like a zombie – a mindless, animated slave to two needy, demanding kids (my hunger, however, is not for human flesh, but for easy recipes with only two canned ingredients) – **Mum A**

I sometimes feel that a walking-talking MumATron has taken up residence in the girl I used to be and stuffed her in a small hole deep inside my body. Every once in a while I hear her screaming to be let out, but there's just no room for her in the tightly scheduled chaos that is my current life – **Mum B**

Last week, I got a little over-excited at the supermarket and bought a small bottle of lime-flavoured milk. It actually felt daring, adventurous and I cackled to myself when I got home and slammed it down on the counter. But there has to be more to life than this. The thrills must exist outside of green milk. There's got to be more to life than a well-hidden Cadbury's Fruit & Nut bar, consumed while you stand at the open cupboard, careful not to crinkle the packaging lest anyone ask what you have there – **Mum C**

Anonymums

Three women, the truth and a whole lot of dares

HarperCollinsPublishers

HarperCollins*Publisher*

First published in Australia in 2011
by HarperCollins*Publishers* Australia Pty Limited
ABN 36 009 913 517
harpercollins.com.au

Copyright © Anonymous 2011

The right of the authors of this work has been asserted
by them under the *Copyright Amendment (Moral Rights) Act 2000*.

This work is copyright. Apart from any use as permitted under the
Copyright Act 1968, no part may be reproduced, copied, scanned, stored
in a retrieval system, recorded, or transmitted, in any form or by any
means, without the prior written permission of the publisher.

HarperCollins*Publishers*
25 Ryde Road, Pymble, Sydney, NSW 2073, Australia
31 View Road, Glenfield, Auckland 0627, New Zealand
A 53, Sector 57, Noida, UP, India
77–85 Fulham Palace Road, London, W6 8JB, United Kingdom
2 Bloor Street East, 20th floor, Toronto, Ontario M4W 1A8, Canada
10 East 53rd Street, New York NY 10022, USA

National Library of Australia Cataloguing-in-Publication data:

Anonymous.
    Anonymums / Anonymous.
    ISBN: 978 0 7322 9169 3 (pbk.)
    Motherhood–Anecdotes.
    Mothers–Anecdotes.
306.8743

Cover design by Priscilla Nielsen, HarperCollins Design Studio
Internal design by HarperCollins Design Studio
Typeset in Hoefler Text 11/15pt by Letter Spaced

For Husbands A, B and C.

Acknowledgments

We would like to thank our husbands (after keeping years of secrets from them, the mind boggles at what we could really get away with) and our children — without them we would have had no material, or grubby prints on the walls. Also, thanks to our agent, Sophie Hamley, our editor Julia Collingwood and everyone at HarperCollins who managed to magically turn our manuscript into a book.

Introduction

There was something wrong with me. The realisation that there was something wrong with me had been creeping up on me for some time, ducking and weaving just out of my view, popping up to tap me on the shoulder and grab my attention when I least expected it. I'd be out somewhere nice with my two kids (a boy and a girl, of course) and my husband (the kind of guy who always changes the toilet roll) – somewhere like the zoo or the park, or out for breakfast. We'd be enjoying ourselves, and then the taunting would start ringing in my head again: 'Why aren't you happy? What are you waiting for? What else is there?'

As the months passed slowly by, I thought about these questions more and more. I was sort of happy. I didn't know what I was waiting for. Was there anything else? I had no idea, but I knew enough to realise that only I was going to provide any answers, so I'd better start looking for them before the voices sent me insane.

The truth was, I knew what the diagnosis would be even before I started searching for one. It was, as Betty Friedan put it, 'the problem that has no name'. And I felt guilty because I believed I had no business feeling less than blissfully happy.

I had everything I could have possibly wanted in life. I had a lovely husband who didn't play golf, indulge in teenage World of Warcraft gaming or expensive Star Wars figurine collecting habits. I had that pigeon pair of children who'd come easily to me, a big home in an affluent suburb, a cleaner, a gardener, enough money to buy pretty close to whatever took my fancy and a flexible job as a writer that kept my brain occupied, but could be dropped at a moment's notice to pick up the slack on the home front (sick kids, sick pets, sick car etc.). Not long ago, one of my friends had gone through the torture of her baby boy dying at 32 weeks and as I watched the tiny coffin slide silently behind the curtains at the funeral home, I felt the stinging shame of every complaint I'd ever uttered about my children and my life, all the while knowing that I'd probably find myself saying more than half of them again.

Most days, I felt like a zombie – a mindless, animated slave to two needy, demanding kids (my hunger, however, was not for human flesh, but for easy recipes with only two canned ingredients). I'd lost any spark I used to have and wondered why my husband still wanted me around. Maybe it was because my undead corpse was cheaper and more labour efficient than hiring a nanny, housekeeper and prostitute. A while back, in a moment of alarming clarity, I'd realised the bars on our front door weren't for keeping people out, they were for keeping me *in*. Still, at least I now knew the reason my expensive eye cream wasn't working – there's only so much Clinique can help you out with when you're the undead.

I zombie-walked a never-ending pattern of events. Prepare meal, gym (work off meal), playground, GP, supermarket, swimming lesson, kindy, day-care, shopping centre, sleep. Nothing else ever seemed to enter the equation. These were

Introduction

the things I did and they were slotted into my life in the correct order on their correct days or the world would fall apart. I squeezed my writing in wherever it would fit. Once a week or so I would service my husband. Not particularly because I wanted to, but because otherwise he'd get grumpy – and grumpy had long-since been claimed as my domain.

Every so often, I'd find myself having strange conversations with women who were my 'kind of' friends, in the way that we'd been brought together only because we'd ovulated at approximately the same time and produced offspring. I'd be sitting with them, cradling a coffee, chatting, when I'd tune in to the conversation and really hear what I was saying. I'd find myself whingeing about the most amazingly middle-class 'I've met way too many of my higher needs, like oxygen, food and water' things. After all, it's only after meeting all the basics and then some that you can really be free to have long and involved discussions on topics like swimming lesson timetabling and tricks for getting around the waiting lists at the best kindergartens. I once had to stop myself mid-whinge when I realised I was complaining about how the cleaning lady had been ironing crooked pleats into my pants (to be fair, she only had one arm). Even more scarily, I realised I was beginning to use the word 'playdate' without flinching.

I caught myself out a few times this way and then started to notice other things. They were mostly little things, but they started to add up.

The first happened when I was out doing the grocery shopping one day and looked down to see 'sponges' written on my list. Nothing too shocking about that, but when I got to the sponges ... I had a preference.

Yes, a sponge preference.

I didn't want to have a sponge preference, I realised with a jolt. Having a sponge preference meant that I'd been domesticated to the point where the chores had taken on meaning.

The second thing was simply depressing. I'd been invited to ... well, let's call it a 'do'. It was a dinner do. It was hosted by my publisher in a very flash restaurant and was of the partnerless variety. I ended up being seated with someone very famous and very smart directly across from me and someone not very famous but also very smart on my right-hand side. On my left-hand side was another someone very famous, but he was only very famous because he'd once done something very stupid and lived to tell the tale, so that, at least, was something. And I needed that something to cling to, because, at the time, I was a full-time breastfeeding mother with a round-the-clock wailing baby and a raging head cold. I got through that dinner but only just – my dignity and self-worth barely crawling out the door of the restaurant at the evening's end. I'd seen the looks when my sleep-deprived and cold-fugged brain couldn't keep up with the conversation. To be fair, everyone was perfectly nice. Perfectly *kind* – in a patronising, 'she's just a mum who does a sideline in writing women's fluff' sort of way.

Just a mum.

I quite liked being a mum, but I'd always dreaded being 'just a' mum. And, now, I was one. Motherhood had taken me up in one big bite and was now swallowing me whole.

It was the third thing, however, that was the deal-breaker. I was slowly going through the process of enrolling my daughter in the same girls' school I'd been to – filling out forms, handing over wads of cash, hoping I'd dressed right for the interview

Introduction

– when in the middle of filling out a form, my pen hovered halfway through writing down which 'house' I'd been in (the information required so my daughter could be siphoned off into the same one). I knew the answer to this question, but something made me pause. I wasn't sure what was wrong, but somehow I wasn't able to continue on with that form.

It took me a while to figure out what I was afraid of.

At first, I thought it must be something about the school – that it wasn't right, or that maybe I was pushing her into going there because I'd been there myself. But I knew that wasn't true. It was the perfect school for her and she'd love it there. So, no, it wasn't the school.

It was me.

By filling out that form, I thought I was lining my daughter up to become ... well, me.

And the bottom line was I wasn't happy with me. The truth was, I could barely remember who 'me' was, anyway.

I had to do something to reclaim my identity. And fast.

It was time to spice things up a bit. To reconnect with whatever was left of me before it was too late.

But how? How to spice things up? A few things I knew for sure. Most importantly, I didn't want to have an affair. I wasn't interested in anything like that. I still kind of liked my husband, even after seven years of marriage. Plus, I had all the sex I wanted on tap. More than I wanted, truth be told. What I wanted was to remember who I used to be BC. Before Children. Even before I was a wife. Back in the days when I was, well ... just me.

Next up, I didn't want to tell anyone about what I was doing. This was going to be just for me. I wanted the frisson-like secret an affair offers, but without the affair. Something

I could think about with a smile while pushing the swing at the park to the cries of, 'higher, Mummy, higher!' Christ, something to get excited about other than whether I'd allow myself to put the mini cheesecakes in the shopping trolley on grocery day.

Finally, I knew that there would be no salsa dancing of any kind. Salsa was the end of the relationship road for me. I'd seen it happen to other people's relationships. When you turn to salsa, it's too late to resuscitate.

In the end, the answer came to me while I was sitting on the couch with my daughter watching Saturday morning kids' TV. The presenters were playing a game, flicking an arrow on a large, round board so it would land on one of two words: Truth or Dare. My daughter asked me to explain what they were doing and my heart paused for a second when I looked up from my newspaper and saw those words: Truth or Dare. Something inside me clicked immediately and wanted to play, too. Mum-style.

A kernel of an idea was formed. Every so often, when I wasn't busy writing 'yoghurt', 'rice crackers' and 'nappies' on the shopping list, I'd go back to it. Think about it. Mull it over. Work on it a little.

I thought about it for months before I made a move. If there were going to be other players involved, I needed them to be just the right type of people. I was sick of playing with most of the mummies on my immediate circuit. They were acquaintances, not friends. For this game, I needed people who wouldn't be scared to tell it like it is. Who wouldn't paint a glossy veneer over the top of their words and thoughts because that's what nice mummies do. But I also couldn't choose people who already knew me well, because they had

Introduction

pre-formed ideas of who I was. It was tricky. And it took what felt like forever to handpick my participants. When I finally did, it took me another forever to get up the courage to do something about inviting them to play.

After yet another mind-numbing day doing the three suburb shuffle (you're not allowed out any further for fear you might keep going), I sent out two cryptic emails to two other mummies I sort of hoped were as bored as I was. Not that I wished unhappiness upon them, but if they were joyously happy, I was about to embarrass myself thoroughly. One of them I had met three times at a writers' conference I went to year after year. Every time we'd met in the past, there had been a spark. We had clicked right from the first minute and were forever laughing – fighting to get the next word in.

The second mum I had never met in person at all, but knew from an online mothers' forum. I'd always admired the brooding snarkiness of her posts, how quick-witted she was and how she was always the first to admit that not everything was happy, happy, joy, joy in her little bubble of motherdom.

Needless to say, it felt more than a bit strange asking two almost total strangers for their phone numbers in order that I could call them and ask if they'd like to play a secret game with me. A three-month secret game, no less. I chose three months because I'd seen this '12-week challenge' poster on the wall at the gym a while back. The poster had mentioned that 12 weeks was long enough to make true changes to your life; habit-forming changes. In this timeframe you could transform yourself and get your life on track. It sounded appealing. And by choosing to transform my mind, rather than my body, I wouldn't have to give up either of my two favourite food groups: alcohol and chocolate. Plus, there was nothing more pitiful than starting out on a project only to have it peter out. Three months we could manage. We could find ourselves in three months, surely? I hoped I wasn't any more lost than that.

So, I rang them both and asked. And, strangely, neither seemed to think it was an odd request at all. Thank God, they were as bored as I was.

We set up a time for our first 'meeting'. As only two of us were based in Sydney, it had to be online. And it had to be private, which was going to be no easy feat. If there weren't children at our feet squabbling like seagulls for yet another peanut butter sandwich, there were husbands whining for their turn on the computer. Privacy, it seemed, was a thing of the past. I was always astounded that in our four-bedroom, three-bathroom house, we could all manage to be in the ensuite at the same time (yes, all six of us, if you included our two cats). But privacy was a necessity if we were to go off big game hunting for the girls we used to be. When the evening arrived, we told our respective lies (I had a phone interview) and closed the doors to our studies firmly behind us.

December

December

the first meeting

Mum A: I hereby call to order the first official Anonymums meeting. I see we all have our secret email accounts up and running. Which means it's now time to talk rules and regulations.

Mum C: I've done my homework!

Mum B: Good girl. You go first then.

Mum C: OK ...
1. Nothing that would make us candidates for *Jackass*. I will not staple a hamster to my genitals.
2. Nothing that would make *us* jackasses. I won't go around telling little children that Santa/The Tooth Fairy/Paris Hilton or any other made-up creatures don't exist.
3. Nothing that would set a jackass *on* us. Road rage is real and I'm only 5'2".

Mum A: Sounds fair to me. And to hamsters.

Mum B: I like Mum C's rules, so I'm only adding two. Anything that requires me to have sex with other men is to be avoided - I like my marriage, and besides I'm too tired. And no jumping out of planes: I will not, repeat not, jump out of planes. Why? Because I think it's so, so, so try hard. You know: 'How am I going to change my life? I know, I'll jump out of a plane!' But what will it change? Nought. NOUGHT!

Mum A: You seem quite definite about that one. No planes, then. My rules are easy. One, nothing sexually deviant. I am not going to any sicko swingers' parties and watching wrinkly old people bump uglies. Two, the truths and dares must revolve around the mum in her natural environment (again, no jumping out of planes, or scaling stupidly large objects). Three, no salsa dancing. Mum B is quite firm on the 'no planes' and I am quite firm on 'no salsa'. Salsa dancing only leads to counselling and then divorce.

Mum C: And don't make me go to scrapbooking classes. I refuse to fall into that chasm of insanely expensive paper and similarly insanely expensive and strangely shaped scissors and hole punches. Not happening.

Mum B: I guess we all have our quirks. So, how do we get started? When?

Mum A: Okay. I say we give ourselves three months. Each week, one person's life will not know what's hit it and will be smacked across the face with both a truth and a dare. So, if Mum B was up first, I could dare her and Mum C could truth her. Mum B could then pass on the baton by truthing me and Mum C could dare me. I could then dare Mum C and Mum B could truth her and so on ... and so on ... around and around we go. We all seem to get into the Sydney CBD now and again, so at the end of each month we'll try to meet up for real and debrief. This means we would do one truth and one dare each per month for three months. Except ...

Mum C: I just knew that there would be an 'except', or maybe a 'but'.

Mum B: Or maybe a, 'You're on Candid Camera!'...

Mum A: Except ... I think we should scrap all that for the last month, February, and do something slightly more daring. For the final month, maybe we should dare *ourselves*. Complete a Big Dare - self-set some crazy task that truly pushes our limits? By that stage we'll all have been examining our lives a little more closely, so why not change something we'd really like to change, or push ourselves a little further, or challenge ourselves personally?

Mum B: I'm still not jumping out of a plane.

Mum C: I might push you out of one if you go on about planes again!

Mum A: No planes, I promise. As for when to get started, how about now?

Mum B: Now is very ... soon.

Mum C: Seeing as this was all your idea, I think Mum B or I should truth and dare you first. I mean, what if this is all an evil ploy to get us to do something stupid so you can forward it on to ten different mothers' forums for a laugh?

Mum A: Of course I'll go first. I'll take a dare to start with. Who's daring me?

Mum B: Mum C can. And then I'll truth you.

Mum C: I'll think of a good one! Possibly involving planes and jumping and some combination of the two.

Mum A: I'll look forward to it! Right. Time's up. Husband is lurking near computer. Must fly ...

December

Mum A

Stats
Age: 34
Height: 163cm and shrinking.
Weight: 59kg on waking; 61kg after the day's excesses
Number of kids: 1 x two-year-old boy, 1 x five-year-old girl (have asked for a vasectomy for Christmas).
Number of husbands: one (would love an extra wife for myself, however).

Okay, I admit I checked my secret email account approximately 500 times over the next few days. It's hard work having a secret email account when nothing is sacred anymore. As soon as the kids see me near the computer, I get hassled. 'I wanna see sharks!' my son tugs on my jeans. He's currently obsessed with watching shark videos on Youtube and I can see we'll have a reluctant beach-swimmer this holiday season. 'Not the 'puter, Mummy.' My daughter tugs on my shirt (she can reach higher) – she hates not having my undivided snack-making attention. 'What are you doing on gmail?' my husband tugs on my ... sanity.

'FFS!' I want to snap at them all. And sometimes I do, because none of them have yet worked out what the acronym means. Not even my husband. I checked once, to see what he might come up with if he Googled the term and had to laugh at him thinking I'd been exclaiming, 'Fédération Française de Ski!' for years, rather than the slightly more obscene, 'For Fuck's Sake!'

Just when I'm about to give up and start checking my email only every few hours, something pops into my In box. Something from someone called Mum C. Immediately my heart freezes, then kicks in again and starts bouncing about in my chest. I'm shocked at my reaction. Already I feel alive and I haven't even read the bloody email yet. I try not to dwell on how sad that is and click 'open'.

To: Mum A
From: Mum C
Subject: Dare

Dearest Mum A,

Seasons greetings! Go down to the local shopping centre, grab yourself a carton of eggnog to get into the spirit of things and then stop into the bottle shop and get something more punchy to slosh into it. You'll need it. Your dare begins by standing in line with a bunch of overtired and overexcited children and their overtired and over-grumpy parents. You will be going up to sit on Santa's knee where you will ask him for a steam mop for Christmas. You must go to the proper, real, middle-of-the-largest-shopping-centre-near-you Santa and not any old chain store,

> B grade Santa. You must sit on his knee (none of that wimpy sitting next to him on the couch business), get photographic evidence and take any sweets/toys offered.
>
> I double dare you to hand one of the photos to your husband and, when he asks why the hell you paid to get them done, tell him you thought that particular Santa was hot.
>
> C.

I must have read that email a good 20 times over. At first to double-check what I thought I'd read and then to look for the sub-text. Was she for real? Go and sit on Santa's knee? How was that life-changing? How was I going to reconnect with the old me in the middle of my local crowded Christmas-crazy shopping centre? Hell, I couldn't find my way from Kmart to Woolies in that place. I was unlikely to find myself.

I didn't reply. And I didn't check my email account for another 24 hours. When I finally did check it again, there was another email waiting for me. It contained only one word.

To: Mum A
From: Mum C
Subject: Dare

> Chicken.

That one word was all I needed. Inside me, the old me piped up from nowhere and said, 'Oi!'

I grabbed my bag, told my husband I needed supplies of feminine hygiene products (they never want any more details) and legged it out the front door. It being the Christmas shopping season, by the time I'd found a car park, I'd lost my gung ho-ho-ho-ness, not to mention about 45 minutes of my life and a whole lot of enamel from my teeth that I'd never get back.

I dawdled my way through the small amount of fabulously exciting shopping I needed to do (Woolies, Kmart, Target ... you know the drill). I slunk by the photographic information booth to find out the prices, which weren't cheap. And I did several reconnaissance missions to check out the queue before I actually lined up. I even asked the elf behind the counter if it was okay for adults to sit on Santa's lap, lest I be ejected from the line after a lengthy wait. The elf, obviously bored, gave me a once over to check out how fat I was and then said, 'Yeah, I guess'. Charming species, elves.

So, with no other shopping left to do and no reason to procrastinate, I took my place at the end of the reasonably long queue and amused myself by working out my heart rate. It was already startlingly high and no-one had even noticed me yet. I started to wonder if I might hyperventilate, or even pass out, as I approached the big red guy himself. At the rate they were pushing people through, that would be my photo – Santa looking down at a spreadeagled, unconscious, me on the floor. Ho, ho, ho, here's your lolly to raise your blood sugar back up to normal levels, now push off, ho, ho, ho.

I kept on queuing and, after a few minutes of my heart rate reaching 120 bpm, I got over myself and started to calm down.

No-one was looking at me at all and the longer I waited, I realised why. Either they were assuming I was with the group in front or the group behind, or they thought my kids were going to pop up beside me at any time – that I was simply the good old 'bag lady', left holding the shopping, securing a place in the long queue while everyone else in the family ducked off to continue living their lives.

The minutes ticked by and, as we slowly but surely progressed forward, I started to attract more and more looks. The sideways glances and whispering began. By the time there were only two groups left in front of me, I was most definitely a beep that was getting louder on the mummy radar. The woman in front of me, with her three kids, pulled them a little closer to her. The woman behind me, with her two kids, took a step back. I was now isolated. A Santa groupie of the too tall tribe. And people walking past, and going up and down the escalators, were beginning to notice me too, now that Mummy of Three and Mummy of Two had stepped aside to leave me shivering by myself in the wintry Christmas cold, singing forlorn 'fa la las' under my breath. Bitches. So much for the Santa Sisterhood.

Finally, I reached the front of the line. And then waited for an eternity as Mummy of Three's kids completely HOGGED Santa's time with their incessant toy-begging (I mean, come on, he's a busy man ... everyone knows you ask for one thing, take the damn lolly and go). They must have run out of things to ask for, because they pushed off eventually and another elf came over to undo the red rope and let me through to the comfort of Santa's red knee. This elf didn't bat an eyelid at my age, but let me through without a second glance. Was I just one of many childless adults that every year lined up to sit on

Santa's knee? This elf had obviously seen it all before. Though, as elves went, she was kind of rough looking – with piercings and so on. She was no snap frozen North Pole fresh looking number.

I walked the walk of 'I'm way too old for this' shame and then I was there. With Him, Santa. He stared up at me with his big blue eyes. 'And what can I do for you, little girl?' he said, licking his lips.

Okay, so he didn't say that and he didn't lick his lips (well, he might have licked his lips underneath his beard – I guess I'll never know). Photographer-elf patted the couch beside Santa. 'You can sit here,' she said.

'But I want to sit on Santa's knee,' I said petulantly, in a tone I'm sure they'd been hearing all day. Plus, Mum C had told me it was the knee or nothing. I didn't want to disappoint on the first dare.

'Of course!' Santa boomed, and patted his right knee. Suddenly, I wasn't quite as keen as Santa seemed to be, but a dare is a dare, so I sucked it up and perched. As it turned out, he was remarkably unfazed to have a 34-year-old woman sitting on his knee. In fact, he was so remarkably unfazed, I wondered what other things had gone on on Santa's knee. Marriage proposals? Romantic trysts?

'Close your legs,' photographer-elf told me, waking me from my daydream. I closed them, red-faced. Goodness. Was I Sharon Stone-ing on Santa's knee? How embarrassing. To cover up for my wantonness, I got straight down to business. 'I'd like a steam mop for Christmas, Santa,' I told him.

'A steam mop? Really?' he said. 'Nothing else?'

'Well, I guess I could also go a Jamie Oliver cookware set and some new Clinique make-up and a Porsche Cayenne –

gold, if it's not too much trouble – and ...' I was starting to realise why the three kids in front of me had taken so long. This was heady, addictive stuff. Since when had I wanted a gold Porsche Cayenne?

'Is that all?' Santa butted in.

'Oh, all that and world peace will do nicely, thanks.'

And with that, a snap, snap of the camera and two crappy lollies, I was booted off Santa's knee unceremoniously by rough-elf, back to the photographic counter. When I got there, bored-elf offered me only photographic packages of $25 and more. It seems elves often 'forget' to tell you you can buy a single photo for $20. Even worse, bored-elf didn't offer me the kiddie toy. I had to *ask* for it, huffily. I made bored-elf line up the toys on the counter (there was a choice of three) and took my time picking the one that most went with my outfit.

Surprisingly, the photos were really good. No earthly idea what I'll do with all eight of them (yes, I got suckered in by bored-elf ...), but they're rather nice.

Santa, if you're reading, my compliments to photographic-elf. But feel free to replace bored- and rough-elves at any time.

P.S. Fulfilled the double dare and gave one of the wallet-sized piccies to my husband. I thought he'd think it was all quite weird and wonder why I'd blown $25 on Santa photos, but he actually thought it was hilarious, and took it to his work Christmas party to hand about. He then proceeded to show it to everyone he'd ever met over the next week (my friends, my family, the postman ...?). Am now thinking I should be a little out there more often if this is the reaction I get. I must have turned truly boring over the past few years judging by his level of excitement.

P.P.S. Santa didn't bring anything on my list. Not even the steam mop, the prick.

*

I was wrong about Mum C's dare. I'd thought sitting on Santa's knee couldn't be life-changing, but it was. To be fair, it was less about Santa and more about taking a step sideways out of my comfort zone, out of the boring everyday routine that I tapdanced week after same-old week. And while that might not have been a big deal for someone else, it was a huge deal for me. Driving home, I felt a strange zingy energy that I hadn't felt for some time. Maybe since uni. A feeling that I'd just done something slightly crazy. Like I'd had a good laugh, even if it was only internal and at myself.

I started to think a bit harder about what my Big Dare might be. The final, self-set one. I'd come up with this Big Dare idea of us daring ourselves for our final round. Instead of being dared by one of the other mums, we would do something bigger and better and scarier by daring ourselves. And then I'd stupidly blurted out this Big Dare idea at our first online meeting. But, so far, I had no idea what my Big Dare might be. I had to try to rustle up something over the coming months, however, because after doing the Santa knee-sit, I could see the dares working for me. This dare thing ...? I'd loved it. And now I wanted more.

But where was I going to get my next fix from? It was only then that I remembered Mum B. There was probably more waiting for me in my In box. Not a dare, that is, but a truth.

I parked the car in the garage, ran inside, dumped my bags, sneakily grabbed the laptop, told my husband I was having 'feminine protection issues' (carrying on the theme) and went and hid in the bathroom.

Thank God for the misunderstood female reproductive system and wireless internet. I sat on the toilet and shakily typed my gmail password three times before I got it right.

Oh, adrenalin. How I'd missed thee.

And there it was. Right where I'd thought it would be.

To: Mum A
From: Mum B
Subject: Truth

A,

Tell me everything about the worst mother you know.

B

When it came to telling all about the 'worst mother' I know, it took me less than three seconds to hit upon who I was going to talk about. Of course, there are plenty of mums I meet on a daily basis who make decisions that I don't agree with: no rules or discipline, preparing four different dinners for four family members, the need to place presents in every layer when playing pass the parcel, no chocolate before the age of five (I always report those last ones to DOCS ...). All of these mothers flitted through my head in those three seconds, until I hit the jackpot – *ka-ching*. Like three sour cherry bunches lining up one after the other, her face appeared in my head and I knew exactly whose tale I was going to tell.

This particular mother is on my mummy circuit, which means I see her all over the place – the shops, the park, the library. Almost every time I see her, she manages to tell me a story about her life that makes my toes curl. I sometimes wonder whether she realises these stories are shocking, or whether she's now so far removed from reality that she has no idea she shouldn't be relating these aspects of her life to other people. Then again, I've heard some of her back story, too, and I'm guessing perhaps her earlier days contained many an interesting and/or painful tale as well. Either way, she always make me want to rush home and hug my family and never let them go.

This woman is married with a young daughter, and two older sons from a previous relationship. Over the past two years or so, she has told me the following things quite light-heartedly:

- Her husband won't let her feed him, or their daughter, anything that's been cooked in the microwave because he doesn't think it's safe, but it's fine by him for her to eat microwaved food and for her two sons to do so, too.
- Her husband won't let her put their daughter into any form of day-care so she can work or study, but they sent her two sons to day-care five days per week (even when she was home looking after their daughter) and now that the boys are at school, they go to after-school care and holiday care during the holidays.
- They are looking into private schooling for their daughter, but her two sons will go to public schools.
- Her husband doesn't like flying with children, so when they fly, she travels with them first and he follows later.
- On the weekends, she has to try to keep the kids out of

the house while her husband 'works' ('working' seems to involve quite a lot of World of Warcraft).
- She's been trying to convince her husband they need a new fridge because the one they have doesn't have any shelves, so the food simply stacks on the bottom of the appliance.

When she tells me these things, I have to admit I don't really know where to look, so I just freeze like a deer in the headlights and listen to what she has to say. Of course, there are plenty of women out there whose husbands have boyish gaming habits, control the money and are slow to shell out for new appliances, but it's the first few things listed that really bother me – the fact that she doesn't seem to realise (or doesn't want to realise? or doesn't care?) that her boys are treated like second-class citizens in their new family.

Having been lucky enough to grow up in a family where my parents are still happily married, I can't even imagine how it must feel to live the life of those boys. And I'm guessing things are only going to get worse. The little girl is still very small, but how is it going to be when all three children fully realise what's going on around them? How will things be between them? What would it be like to watch your younger sister leave for school in her fancy blazer knowing that your mum and stepfather were dropping $15,000 a year on her education and nothing close to that on yours? To have your mother ferry you off to holiday care while your sister stayed home? To be taken out every weekend not for the pleasure of your company but because you were unwelcome in your own home?

Recently, it's the younger boy who's been bothering me more than his mother. I find myself trying to avoid this mum and her kids; actively not going places when I think they might be there. When I first saw the younger boy a few years ago, I thought he was a lovely thing – all hair that stood straight up and gloriously gangly. But now all I can see is his desperate need for attention and how if I give him any, he's suddenly all over me, wanting more, taking more, clambering all over me. I find I have to prise myself away because I know I'll never be able to give him what he needs, which is probably just a simple feeling of belonging – of knowing he's wanted and cherished not just by his mother, but by everyone in his family. I'm ashamed to say that this feeling of needing to distance myself became so strong that when the mother kindly gave me a bag of her younger son's outgrown clothes a year or so ago, I found I couldn't put them on my own child; that those clothes actually made me feel a bit ill. I put them in the back of the linen cupboard and forgot about them ... until a few days ago.

Mum B's truth made me remember them. They are the one link in my house to this mother and her kids, and I found myself fishing them out again. As I unpacked the bag and looked at the clothes before me, I knew I was being silly and stupid, not letting my son have them (he loved a good cast-off from a 'big boy'), but still ... I couldn't do it. I couldn't put my son in them. Wanting them out of my sight, I quickly decided to pass them on to another girlfriend who didn't know what I knew. I was just about to put them in the car, so I wouldn't forget to give them to my friend on our next visit, when something made me pause. I'm not sure what it was, but, in that moment, I realised there was more to this situation than I'd previously recognised. Mum B's truth had challenged me to stop and really think about this mother I knew, when normally I would rush through any thoughts I had of her. Now, I stopped to question my every feeling about her. There had to be something else about this woman ... but I couldn't figure it out and it took another few days until it became clear to me why I always had such a strong, physical reaction to her. As it turned out, it was very simple.

She scared the living shit out of me.

Once I realised it was fear that was setting me off, it was then easy to work out exactly why it was she scared me. She scared me because I didn't know how many steps away I was from being in her position. She scared me because, deep down, I knew she wasn't a bad mother – she was a good mother in a bad situation.

And that could so, so easily be me. Be any of us, really.

That was why I couldn't bear to be around her. Because she was a reminder of how I could be a 'bad' mum too. That I was maybe only a few decisions away from being the 'worst' mum on someone else's radar.

When I realised this, I fished those clothes out once more and looked at them as I remembered something else she'd told me. She had been a single working mum when her sons were tiny and it had been hard. Really hard. When she told me this, months back, all I could do was stand there and look at her blankly and wonder that surely that must have been preferable to what she'd ended up doing – marrying her current husband. A guy who left a lot to be desired. But maybe it *was* that hard? How would I know? I'd been lucky enough to marry the guy of my dreams, who was so laidback, he asked *me* for pocket money. I'd never had to make the hard choices because I'd been lucky enough not to have been dealt any rotten cards. Hell, I could walk out the door right now and buy *myself* a new fridge if I wanted (whee ...).

Which also got me to wondering, what would I do if I suddenly didn't have so many choices? If my husband came home right now and said he wanted a divorce, packed a suitcase and left? I mean, what would I really *do*? I guess I'd probably have to take the kids and stay with my parents for a bit while we packed up the house mid-lease. Then I'd find a small apartment for us all and move into that. But how much money would we have? Would I have to get a full-time job? What on earth would I do? What was I good for? And how would that work with the schools we'd chosen and drop-offs and pick-ups and so on? I could bet on one thing, though ... it would be hard. Really hard.

And maybe that was what happened to that 'worst' mum I knew. Maybe she started out making a few small concessions in the hope of giving herself and her sons a better life, and then didn't notice she was sliding down a slippery slope? I'd been so self-righteous thinking I could never make the choices she'd made for my daughter or my son, but could I?

All I could do was cross my fingers and hope I'd never know.

One thing I do know, though – I won't be avoiding her anymore. And I'm keeping the bag of clothes. My son can wear them anytime he wants.

*

I was glad it was still almost a good three weeks until our first anonymums real-life debrief, because I was so ashamed of myself. I was a judgment passer of the worst kind – on another mother. I was hoping I'd recover in time to be able to show my face, but I wasn't sure. In the hope of taking the limelight off me after my truth had been circulated to Mums B and C, I tried to think quick. How could I take Mum B out of her comfort zone in the same way I'd been taken out of mine? It took me a few days and a little email colluding with Mum C to work it out, but I did it.

As I pressed 'send', I wished Mum B good luck ... she was going to need it.

Anonymums

Mum B

Stats

Age: 39

Height: 175 cm - my collection of flats is almost as extensive as Nicole Kidman's was during the Cruise years.

Weight: Can I just say 'challenged'?

Number of kids: Two: Big Boy (four) and Little Boy (one). Any possibility of a third is sliding off the table as fast as a one-year-old's Weetbix.

Number of husbands: Just the one, thanks.

Nobody told me there'd be days like these.

Oh, they tried. When I was pregnant, friends winked knowingly and muttered stuff about 'no life, no sex, no fun', but I, in my all-knowing, all-seeing, all-glowing pre-maternal state knew that I'd be different. My child would simply fit in with what I wanted to do. My husband would never complain about lack of sex. And how could hanging out with a beautiful cherub, watching him/her explore the world while sipping a latte, not be fun?

Fast-forward four years and cue 'I told you so'. The trouble is, nobody can really tell you. I watch new mums gnash their teeth, throw their arms in the air (flashing their brand-new mummy tummies to the world) and wail 'why didn't somebody tell me it would be like this?' Well, sugar, we did. But you were going to be different, remember?

It's all so easy in hindsight.

Now I find myself considering wasting one of my Three Magic Wishes on a washing-up fairy. When I was young – that is, before children – had a genie puffed out of a bottle offering me the three things I most desired, I'd have gone for money, sex and chocolate. Now – and I think about this a lot – it's all about chores, babysitting and, oh yes, chocolate.

See what my life has become? Two kids under four and the world is your oyster shell – closed, dark and depressing, with an underlying stench of total boredom.

It didn't used to be this way. I had an okay job in publishing. I enjoyed sampling cuisine, fine and otherwise, at various restaurants, and was, I like to think, regarded as a good-time gal with a smart line and an enormous capacity for alcohol. I was a girl who knew how to have fun.

I still have a job in publishing that I now wedge around being a full-time mum. I occasionally go to the nearest pub for a Noice Bistro Meal with the family. These days when I drink (not often – I feel as though I've been pregnant or breastfeeding for the last century), I have one or two and drink four glasses of water after each. Anything to stave off the horror of being left at home alone with two kids and a hangover.

To say I'm desperate for change is a mild understatement. It's not that I don't love the kids and the husband and the cute little cottage in which we live. I even enjoy the gardening and home-making (though not, I think I've made clear, the day-to-day drudgery). It's just that I sometimes feel that a walking-talking MumATron has taken up residence in the girl I used to be and stuffed her in a small hole deep inside my body. Every once in a while I hear her screaming to be let out, but there's just no room for her in the tightly scheduled chaos that is my current life.

So when I stumbled across Mum A's invitation, it wasn't even a case of 'what the hell?' but more a, 'hell yes!' I had only one proviso: I won't be called a mummy. Mummies – yummy and otherwise – might be taking over the world, with their Seven For All Mankind jeans, their pedicures and their $2500 Stokke prams, but I will not join them. I am a mum.

To me, 'mummy' has angst-ridden, anxious, helicopter parent written all over it. Mums, on the other hand, are dependable, salt-of-the-earth, wise creatures.

Mummies might provide Planet Cake cupcakes and a Fiona Scanlan fairy costume for the preschool Christmas party, but mums can do amazing things with self-raising flour and a bit of tinfoil. I confess that I am not quite there yet – my self-raising flour frequently refuses to rise and I had to send my oldest to the last fancy dress party as an 'Olympian' (white baby wrap, cardboard medal, plastic wreath) due to my underwhelming sewing skills. But I have aspirations. And there is no 'my' on the end of them.

Phew, glad I've got that out of the way. Don't mind me if I go off on random tangents at times. I think it's one of those things that comes with the licence to parent. What do you mean, you didn't get one of those? Nobody does, and don't you think that's half the trouble?

These days you need a licence to fish. You need a licence to boat. You need to do about 1000 practice hours before you get a licence to drive (and aren't we all hoping there'll be someone else around to undertake that task when the kids are 16 and yearning to hit the road?).

And yet they'll let you out of a hospital with a newborn baby and a fandangled safety capsule that won't, simply will not, fit back in the car like it's supposed to. You don't even have to sign anything. I remember hubby and I looking sideways at each other as we crept towards the lift, gingerly holding our bundle of joy in a plastic gondola, waiting for someone to stop us, anyone. I looked down at my crinkled little newborn baby and whispered, 'Don't worry, your real parents will be here to pick you up any minute now ...'

But I digress yet again. See what I mean?

What else do you need to know about me? My favourite colour? Changes daily. I used to be so fixed about these things and then I spent time with a toddler. A toddler whose favourite colour changes hourly depending on which Wiggle is top of his Christmas card list at that time. Initially, it drove me nuts. I mean, you either have a favourite or you don't. Now I'm more flexible. I have come to realise the joys of loving blue one minute and being totally into hot pink the next.

Actually, I think that flexibility is one of those pluses of parenting that nobody ever gets around to mentioning. Yep, just as nobody tells you how hard it will be, nobody really gets into the good stuff either. The trouble is that it all gets a bit Johnson & Johnson ad when you try to explain that your favourite shade of green is that 'misty forest' colour that your son's eyes take on when he wears a dark green shirt. Or that the softest place in the world is that little crook in a baby's neck. Or that everybody would want cellulite if they looked as good in layer upon layer of fat as your eight-month-old baby.

See what I mean? Already your stomach is turning. But I try really hard to embrace the good stuff because it helps hide the pain of suppressing the rest. The truth of the matter is that I reckon that raising children is boring; important, but boring. It doesn't matter how many times you go Round the Mulberry Bush, All Fall Down, or Rock A Bye Your Bear in a day, the fact is that you have to get up the next day and do the whole damn lot again. In between dealing with other people's bodily fluids (and solids), keeping the place vaguely clean, paying the bills, stressing over illnesses, stressing over development, stressing over work, stressing over the fact that you're not svelte six minutes after the birth, stressing over the fact that you're not engaging in acrobatic sex at least three times a week and stressing about whether you've Let Yourself Go. It's enough to make a person want to Let Herself Go.

But we don't, do we? Or at least we try not to. Instead we attempt to keep up the charade that we have everything under control and everything we want.

Half the time we don't even know what the hell we want. Just that it probably isn't this.

I read Virginia Woolf's *A Room of One's Own* and I want one. I have a husband who could build me one, but I wouldn't have time to go there so I resist the temptation. Having my own space sitting empty, mocking me, would be worse than having no space at all. (And the truth is that it would be better served as a playroom. At least then I'd be able to walk across a room without getting Duplo men embedded in my feet.)

The thing is, I'm good at truths. Truths as I see them anyway. So when I heard I was up for the truth part of this first challenge, I relaxed a little. I can talk. I can be honest. How hard can this be?

December

To: Mum B
From: Mum A
Subject: Truth

Dear B,

My dare and truth are done. Now, are you ready? I hope not, because I'm beginning to think it's going to be a lot more fun that way …

You will tell the truth about your most used sexual fantasy. I'm not talking about that deep yearning dream you have that he'll just roll over and go to sleep. No, we want to know about the other sort, the sort that makes you not care what that noise is, makes you forget about that model volcano you must make by Tuesday, makes you stop making mental notes to buy more Domestos, pipe cleaners and back-to-school book covers. We want the sort that gets the ol' engine revving and entrenches you in 'the moment'.

Don't hold back. But be warned, if they involve Domestos, pipe cleaners and back-to-school book covers, it's a fantasy fail.

A

I have to confess that I often wonder about other people's sex lives. Not about the 10 per cent* of people who reckon they bonk every night of the week, but about people I meet regularly for a monthly dinner. Do they go home after we've had dinner together and get it o-o-nn? Sick, I know. One minute I'm serving them sticky date pudding and ice cream, the next I'm contemplating the stickiest part of their relationship. If only they knew.

One thing I don't do is actually *picture* them together. That would be just plain icky. Plus I'm not really a particularly visual type of person. Porn films of the 'I've come to clean the pool' variety just don't do it for me. I tend to get bogged down in the details – how exactly is he going to get *that* into her? – and lose sight of the overall apparent horniness of it all. They seem like a surgical exercise to me, or perhaps I've just seen the wrong ones.

I can still remember the first orgasm I ever had. I was 11 years old, had an irritation from a pair of size-too-small knickers, tried a quick rearrangement and a bit of a scratch before going to sleep and hey presto! I was up all night, feverishly chasing that amazing sensation. I mean *all* night, over and over again. I could barely walk the next day and could hardly wait to get into bed again.

Which is where I suffered my first disappointment. So irritated was I from the previous night's activities that it was all pain, no gain. I learned a couple of valuable lessons.

1. The best way to learn your body's capacity is to find out for yourself.
2. Quit while you're ahead and live to come another day.

* *All figures based on anecdotal evidence and from what I can remember reading in women's magazines while waiting for our GP.*

December

When I first began sleeping with guys, I suffered my second, crushing disappointment. Nobody, it seemed, understood my buttons like I did. Oh sure, there was a lot of nice kissing and some lovely stroking and even some assured lovemaking, but it seemed that I was one of *Cosmo* magazines 30 per cent of women who never orgasm. Which, of course, I knew was not true. And I had the callouses to prove it. (I never did get into vibrators, preferring a more manual approach.)

I broached the subject with a couple of close friends. One showed a dominatrix side I'd never have suspected when she admitted that she always insisted on coming first. She'd basically just do whatever the hell it was she had to do to get there before she'd let her partner 'take his pleasure' (her words, not mine).

'You've got to get on top,' she instructed. So I tried that. My boyfriend at the time was more than happy to let me do all the work up there. Trouble was, it got him so worked up that he'd explode before I'd even got comfy in my seat. He'd be all 'oh baby' and I'd be 'oh crap'.

The second friend I blushingly asked agreed that it was almost impossible for a woman to orgasm through the normal machinations of sex.

'It's all about the tongue,' she said, wiggling hers for effect.

'You mean I should tell them what I want?' said I, hoping that's what she meant.

Her look was pitying. 'No, you moron, I mean oral sex.'

Right. I have to admit I've never been a huge fan of licky sex. It all just seemed so ... moist. And so few men actually know what they're doing down there. Half of them give you a half-hearted sniff, the other half are incredibly enthusiastic – to the point of basically irrigating the area. Eeuucch.

Having dumped the aforementioned boyfriend I gave it another try and advanced on a mission to find a rebound affair. In fact, I picked a guy who'd been discussed in various circles as being pretty good at it. We had a few beers, a casual grope and almost before I knew it, he was paying homage at the altar of my Goddess.

Let's just say that the waves didn't crash on the beach. In fact, I was so bored after a few minutes and so tired (little did I know that this was good training for my post-baby life) that I pulled him on top of me in a fit of faux passion just to get it over with. (This truth stuff is good therapy. I'm remembering that my sex life prior to marriage and children wasn't all Hollywood soft focus. If you'd asked me about it prior to this, I'd have said it was one long montage of chocolate body paint and Sunday afternoons in bed.)

I gave it one more try. This time I tried a more alternative approach, seeking out my one slightly hippy mate. I thought she'd suggest essential oils and meditation, maybe even tantra, but she was much more literal. 'I like to read erotica before I start,' she said.

Erotica. 'You mean like Mills & Boon sex scenes?' I was already au fait with the guilty pleasure of the well-thumbed 'reunion' scene in many a romance novel. In fact, I found them great fodder for self-fondling. I had a friend who set out to write one once – she stopped when she realised that women the world over might be masturbating to her masterpiece.

'Well, you could start with that if you wanted ...' she said, clearly implying I was setting my sights too low. 'Actually, I'd start with anything written by Anais Nin, or the *Story of O*.'

'But what do you do with them? Read them before you go out and then look for someone to enact them?'

'No, you moron,' she said. (I was beginning to question the validity of my friendships at this point.) 'We read them to each other.'

I thought of Susan Sarandon making that young guy read her poetry in *Bull Durham*. This might work. I left her house that day with a pile of books.

Which brings me to the point of this truth: my favourite sexual fantasy. The truth is that I have lots.

I read somewhere that the favoured fantasy of most women was a rape scenario. I find this so hard to believe. One, because I came a little too close to the real thing once. Mostly, though, because there are so many other more creative outlets out there. Thanks to the writer Anais Nin, for instance, I have the pleasure of imagining myself being anonymously felt up on a train. Or with two other women in a sea of hands and exotic French accents. Or riding bareback, naked, in the forest with only a saddle horn for company.

I can be fucked by a well-hung Russian while my husband watches in a lather of expectation. (In a fantasy, even a well-educated, good-role-model mum can say fuck.) Interestingly, none of my fantasy fucks has a well-known face. I've never taken Brad, or George, or Hugh, or any other celluloid creature to bed.

I wandered into Nancy Friday's *My Secret Garden* once and was happy to find that she believes that fantasy doesn't necessarily equal secret wish fulfilment. I love the idea of lying motionless, pretending to sleep, while a man takes advantage of me. In reality, I'm ticklish and hate the idea of being taken advantage of – no matter how pleasurable.

Fantasies are funny like that. When I was younger, I used to fantasise about sleeping with a black man. I had dreams of cocoa skin on silky white sheets; the feel of a carpet of short curly hair; the thrill of huge dark hands on my own fair flesh ...

Then I slept with one, and discovered that, beyond the Film Noir experience of a monochrome adventure, it was much the same as with the blonds, the redheads and the brunettes I'd tried in the past. Chalk it up to experience and move on to a new fantasy.

Sometimes, however, acting out works a treat.

When I was pregnant the second time I was the horniest I have ever been in my life. I found myself trawling the internet for inspiration. I found none. Well, not much anyway. Most of what's out there is deeply boring. Plus, it's hard to get in the mood when you're sitting in front of a 100W screen. I don't know how all those cybersexual weirdos do it.

I returned to my library. One story that did it for me every single time was a strange little tale written 100 years ago about a French (are you sensing a theme here?) countess who hired young men, took them home and sucked them dry, literally. She was the mistress of oral sex, taunting and teasing them for hours on end. Why? Because the only way she could get off herself was to perform fellatio whilst pleasuring herself.

The story is told from the point of view of one of her young victims. So it's a wholly male affair. And yet the idea of being such an expert was so tantalising that I took to the idea with gusto – and no complaints from Husband B.

So there it is. More of my fantasy life than you ever wanted to know – and I ever thought I'd tell. The beauty of fantasy is that it works when you are on your own or with friends. I can use Anais's inspiration in those moments when I'm in bed and the grocery list and other mundane 'must-dos' threaten to intervene in my pleasure. Or I can use her as a kick-start when I just need a little solo R&R.

I brought up the topic of masturbation at a hen's party once – as you do. Of the 10 women there, five nodded sagely when I said that I often used it as a cure for insomnia. The other five looked at me as though I'd just offered to perform a Brazilian on myself as after-dinner entertainment. They'd never tried it, they admitted, after a little (okay a lot of) persuasion.

Anyway, it's late, the dishes are unwashed (where's that damn fairy when you need her?), the lunches are unmade and Big Boy needs a button mended on his favourite shirt.

I have a new fantasy. It entails a nanny, a cleaner and a cook. I'll tell you all about it next time ...

*

24 hours later ...

I still can't quite believe that I entrusted my most intimate thoughts to cyberspace. I'm glad nobody knows who Mum B is. It feels delicious to have an alter-ego. There's freedom in invisibility.

I've never really understood the online gaming thing – avatars and all that – but I'm beginning to get the idea. Building a new personality from scratch is liberating and, let's face it, empowering. God built the world in seven days and I created Mum B in seven pages, or thereabouts.

I confess that sharing my sexual fantasies did send me to bed feeling amorous. Having thought out loud about them, I approached my husband with renewed interest. Generally our sex life is about what you'd expect with two kids – in fits and starts, with him more interested than me in getting things going. After the first baby I made a real effort to keep up my end, so to speak. I was determined not to become a statistic. I didn't want to be one of those women who sat around talking about how they never had sex anymore. I like sex. I used to like it more, when I had time, sleep and a flat stomach. But I'm still quite fond of it.

After two kids, though, I had to stop pretending that I still had the energy of a childfree woman. Sleep deprivation is the biggest passion killer on the planet, bar none. When I saw sheets, I didn't think of horizontal dancing, I just thought of being horizontal.

I have new resolve, though. Sharing my truth has shown me one thing: the truth is that I'm still a woman with sexy thoughts. I can still be a sexy woman. I can still be a woman with a sex life.

Sometimes you just need to step back from your daily existence and think about how you live. I choose to live a close, intimate life with my man. I will just have to work out how to fit it into family life.

I'm just starting to wonder what Mum C has in store for me, when I find in my emails ...

To: Mum B
From: Mum C
Subject: Dare

Dearest Sexy Siren,

Red hot fantasies are made to be coupled with red hot lips. You will spend a week, a whole week, in red

> lipstick. Full red, pouty lips; no tints, no glosses. We want a sexy screen siren of the old Hollywood era leaving her thick, waxy mark everywhere.
>
> Smear it on from dawn to bedtime and tell us everything. How does it make you feel? Did people notice? Did they comment? What did they say? What about your husband? Does he like it? Are you tempted to leave big kissy-lips stains on his collar?
>
> Have fun with it!
>
> Your dear friend,
>
> Mum C

First disclosure: I am *not* a red lipstick kind of a girl. In fact, I'm not really a make-up kind of a girl. Most days I manage tinted moisturiser. On a good day, I get carried away with a bit of mascara and, gasp, a lip gloss. But those days are rare. So this is not so much a dare for me as a red hot challenge.

I approach with caution.

Second disclosure: In an attempt to bond with my alter-ego sex pot Mum B, I gave my boring brown hair a light copper rinse a few weeks ago. I asked my husband if it made me look sexier. He looked me over and said it made me look paler. In my mind, I was immediately Nicole Kidman, all alabaster skin and glossy copper curls. I should have stopped right there.

But no, I made the mistake of asking him if my new look made him think differently of me. He admitted that he'd never been able to look at a redhead without wondering if she had ginger pubes. So, yeah, he was looking at me differently; wondering if the fireplace matched the mantel. The cuffs matched the collar, the ... well, you get what I'm saying.

Visions of Nicole, Katharine Hepburn, even Jessica Rabbit marched out of my head, replaced by a nerdy redhead who needed a touch of the sun and wore a t-shirt with the slogan 'Possible Ginger Muff'.

Now this.

The trouble with my new red hair – apart from the above – is that red hair and red lipstick are not renowned for being a match made in heaven. One thing about boring brown is that it doesn't tend to clash with anything. It's not exciting, but it ain't difficult either.

So my first challenge is to actually find a red lipstick that I can stand wearing for seven days, 24 hours a day. It's not easy.

My first stop is the local chemist where I find three budget beauty brands and about 33 shades of red. I try them all. By the time I leave the shop, I have 27 orangey red smears up my arms, three berry red smears on my cheeks where I've tried to wipe them off my lips with a tissue and succeeded in blending them all over my face, and three shades on the backs of my hands that the assistant assures me are Blue Red, and therefore perfect for me.

I'm not convinced.

Clearly, this is going to need a more upmarket outing. I plan with care, visions of gorgeous gold Estee Lauder, luxurious black Chanel, even clinical green Clinique dancing in my head. On the day of my excursion, it pours with rain, Little Boy has gastro, Big Boy wants to watch *Sesame Street*, and, frankly, I'm over it before it begins.

So much for glamour.

I turn to every mum's best friend, the internet. Thanks to Google, I discover www.justforredheads.com – an entire beauty range formulated for my rouge sisters. I have to say that the earthy tones are gorgeous and would look equally good on a chick with hair of less spectacular hue (which will be me when the rinse wears off), but there's no vibrant red lipstick (this should tell me something, right?), so I move on.

I find a beauty website, featuring a lovely photo of the girl in charge and, underneath, a little invitation to ask her anything. I take up her up on it and send off an email asking for the one shade of red that will suit all redheads.

She recommends Mac Dubonnet and, putting all my trust in her smiling 'About Me' picture, I head to the Mac website and order one. While I'm there, I pick up a new Mac Spice lip pencil because, according to my beauty friend, one should never try to put red lipstick on naked lips. Already I am more high maintenance than I was before this exercise began. I have a bad feeling things can only get worse.

Day 1

When the small black box arrives on my doorstep at lunchtime on Friday, I can't even bring myself to open it. To do so means the dare begins. Much better to put that off until later. After all, everything looks better when the light's a little lower, right?

By 7pm, I can put it off no longer. I am no shirker, no dare-avoider. Hiding in the kitchen under the auspices of preparing dinner, I pick off the sticky tape, open the lid and peer inside.

There, between environment-destroying (but oh so inviting) layers of black tissue paper lies an innocuous black tube and a pencil.

I grab the tube, pop the top – hey presto, a luscious, deep, dark, sexy, intense, seductive, and very scary lipstick is nestled inside.

I'm standing above an abyss. Part of me wants to put it back in the box and forget the whole thing. My clothes, my face, my *life* are not up to this lipstick. People who wear colours like this wear heels and skirts and lacy lingerie, for heaven's sake. They do not think that 'dressing up' involves cargo pants and, possibly, a shirt that requires ironing. They do not spend their lives picking up toys, emptying sand from pockets and changing nappies. They have 'people' who do all that for them.

What was that I said about being a 'no shirker', 'no dare-avoider'? Oh yes.

Before I can think too much, I am in the bathroom, under the 100W (energy efficient) globe, carefully feathering Mac Spice over my lips (I figure I'm going to need all the help I can get). Winding up the tube of lipstick, I run it over my lips. I smack them together and stand back to survey the effect. All I can see are the bits I've missed. Trying again, I carefully fill in the gaps, trying not to go outside the lines. It proves impossible. I have Bozo lips.

Grabbing a sheet of toilet paper, I wipe it off and start again.

Three attempts later, I'm back in the kitchen, serving up dinner. Husband B wanders in as I'm putting the final peas on the plates. His double-take gives him whiplash.

'Going somewhere?' he manages.

'Dressed like this?' I answer, aiming for nonchalance. He looks me over. Takes in the hot pink pyjamas dotted with cartoon sheep. Now he's really confused.

'Why are your lips so red?'

'I'm, um, trying a new signature look.'

'A what?'

'You know, a signature look – something I wear all the time and everyone associates with me.'

Silence. 'Like Bozo the clown?'

Sigh. It's hard to be offended when you agree. 'Something like that.'

He looks me over again. 'Lose the pyjamas and you might get somewhere.'

I smile. My seductive lipstick is working already!

He continues: 'Dinner ready? Let's eat, I'm starving.'

So much for hot kitchen sex. I sit at the table and watch my seductive lipstick smear itself all over my glass, the prongs of my fork, my napkin ... Yep, those women who wear this sort of colour definitely have 'people' who clean up after them.

Day 2

It's 8am and I'm watching Big Boy attempt to kick his way across a two-metre stretch of pool without drinking the contents of said pool. He's still smiling, so drowning can't be too imminent.

Public humiliation, however, is already upon me. I'm wearing tracksuit pants, a t-shirt (it's 100 degrees in this greenhouse – my pores are squeaky clean) and the Dubonnet. I refreshed it as soon as I woke up, so as not to have too much time to think about it. If I thought it was bright last night, it's blinding this morning. Sleepy, puffy skin does not need this level of contrast.

By the time I got to the pool, though, I'd forgotten I had it on. Until I smiled at the receptionist, who looked at me as though I'd grown another head. Apparently they don't see too much screen-siren red at the pool. Particularly not at that time of the morning.

When I took Big Boy over to the side of the pool to endure the usual 'why, Mummy, oh why, do I have to get in?' performance, the teacher looked up at me from her watery empire with even more pity than usual. She's used to Big Boy's histrionics. The sight of his mum with technicolour lips was far more off-putting.

My parent cohort on the side of the pool is sneaking sideways glances at me. I don't know how much of this I'm going to be able to take. I return my gaze to Big Boy's thrashing progress, thinking that if I focus on him, I might feel less self-conscious. But I can't help but wonder whether every single person I meet this week will treat me like a freak of nature.

I'm getting a headache just thinking about it. Or perhaps it's the reflected glare from my lips ...

7pm
I'm waiting for a 'fashion forward' friend in the foyer of the local multiplex cinema. I've primed her for the meeting, using the 'new signature look' approach. Given that her look changes as often as I change Little Boy's nappies, she is unsurprised. Her reaction? 'It suits you, you should rock that look more often.' No more is said.

Day 3

I have to admit I'm flabbergasted. Not a word I use often, but the only verb suitable for the occasion. Today I have seen not one, not two, but three members of my immediate family: people who know me well; people who are not renowned for being backward in coming forward; people from whom I expected to receive a merciless ribbing for my glamorous new look.

No-one said a word.

Not a word.

Not even a vague acknowledgment.

Even after I left a love-you-long-time red kiss mark on each and every cheek.

Either they were so pleased to see me looking a bit groomed that they decided to let the moment pass, or I am so much wallpaper in everyone's lives, they didn't even notice.

I choose to believe the former.

After all, I *had* made a special effort. I realised yesterday at the pool that I didn't have the nonchalant chic that would allow me to pull off the red-lips-with-trackies effect that celebs manage with aplomb. Nope. In everyday life, red lips demand that you rise to the occasion – even if there's no occasion.

So I wear base. I wear mascara. I wear a little neutral, no-make-up-style eye shadow. I put product in my hair each day, so that I don't end up just dragging it into a pony tail.

Remember I said I didn't have the life to go with red lips? Well, it turns out that the red lips dictate that my life falls into line. They demand that I dress up, at least a little.

Don't get me wrong. It's not like I'm the sort of person who would ever Let Myself Go. I wax. I dye. I exercise in the vague hope that one day the mummy tummy will reduce.

Perhaps I am guilty, though, of letting things drift a bit. Generally, I choose comfort over style, and red lips is definitely not a comfort option.

I am scrambling to keep up.

Days 4, 5 and 6

I could kid myself (and you) that every day of my existence is new and exciting since I began with the red lipstick. But the routine must remain in place or the family wheels will fall off.

I might look as though I'm ready to jet off to Paris at a moment's notice – particularly now that I've traded in my trainers for leather boots, my cargo pants for nice dark denims and my T-shirts for ... well, I'm still wearing those, but I've dragged a fitted, chocolate brown jacket from the depths of the wardrobe to pull the look together – but in reality I'm just schlepping from day-care, to work, to the supermarket, to playdates, to the stove, to the sink, to bed.

The funny thing is, I do feel different in ways both good and bad.

On the downside, I'm not kissing my kids as much – not only do they end up looking like extras in a B-grade slash flick, but I have to keep re-applying. The re-applying is killing me. When you're a low-maintenance lip-gloss-on-a-good-day girl, the constant maintenance needed to keep red lips looking hot, sexy and kissable is a real eye-opener. This became horribly apparent on Day 4 at the office, when I went to the bathrooms at 2pm and realised I hadn't re-applied since 8am. With a thin red line around the outside of my lips, I looked plain scary.

On the plus side, I feel fantastic putting on my lips. Now that I'm over the shock of the colour (and the headaches are subsiding), I can fully appreciate the lift it gives my face. Not only that, but my teeth look whiter.

I'm not sure that I'd call it confidence, but red lips certainly put a spring in your step. Actually, make that a saunter.

Husband B has watched confused and bemused as the days have unfolded. By Day 4, he'd stopped enquiring whether I'd finished writing my 'signature'. When my red-lipped self appeared strumpet-like at the end of the bed where he lay reading and proceeded to, well, put some lipstick on his collar, he was a convert. No more Bozo comments. All I have to do is lick my red lips in his direction and he's putty in my hands. I could get used to this. Except all that licking leads to more re-applying.

There's a price to pay for everything.

Day 7

Last day of the dare and I'm torn. Half of me is so relieved it's over that I want to consign this high-maintenance regimen to the hell from which it came (or at least the bottom drawer of the bathroom cabinet). The other half of me clings to my little tube of glamour like a baby koala clings to Mama.

Such a small thing, a shade of lipstick, but it can have such a huge impact on your day. There were mornings – and we all have them – when I looked in the mirror at my pale, worn-out face, with its window boxes of under-eye bags, trying to clean my teeth while Little Boy clutched at my pyjama pants and Big Boy tried to work out whether his thumb would fit up the spout, thinking 'what in God's name am I doing with my life?' I'd sigh, reach for my lipstick and, voila, a heart-shaped mouth that looked as though it was *going somewhere* looked back at me.

When you're feeling stuck, that's sometimes all the push you need.

Day 8

'You look different today.'

Husband B has taken a pause from his favourite activity – rummaging through the fridge – to examine me from head to toe. He takes in the unofficial uniform – yep, back to cargo pants, trainers etc. – and cocks an eyebrow.

'What happened to the new signature?' he enquires.

'I decided it wasn't really me.'

'Oh.'

He turns to rummage some more, emerging moments later with what looks like the entire contents of the local deli in his hands.

'I kind of liked it,' he continues, as though the rummage never happened.

'Liked what?' I say, confused. Is he talking about salami?

'The signature. The red.'

'Oh.' I pause. 'I thought you hated it.'

'Well, it was a bit much with trackies and pyjamas, but I didn't mind it when we went out. It looked ... dressy.'

Dressy. Not sexy or cool or seductive or screen-siren. But that's okay. Dressy has its moments.

So I have not retired the Dubonnet. No dusty bottom

drawer for its siren songs. Instead, I'm saving it for special occasions.

And I've decided to make lots more of those.

*

I need a full-on beauty and fashion makeover. So that's what I'm doing. I started with the make-up bag, throwing out the four-year-old eye shadows, the 'not-quite-right' foundation, and the mascara that I'm sure I've had since 2003. I'm left with what's kindly known as 'the basics', but that's okay. I've booked a sitter (okay, my mum) and I'm heading to the most glamorous beauty counter I can find to upgrade my kit. Except for my dusky-pink lipstick, of course, which I've worn for the last two years simply because it's fabulous. And I will never give up the Dubonnet, which will be working back with black-on-black this very Saturday night.

As for the clothes, I'm moving a little more slowly. I've dumped the couture collection of tracksuit pants I've had 'just in case' since Big Boy was born. There will be no occasion that deserves those ugly things. I've weeded out the 'comfy' stuff that I've been holding on to despite the fact that it's torn or stained or just plain unwearable. But a new wardrobe is a big investment. I'm starting with shoes – as every woman does, simply because she knows her size will never change.

But before I hit the shops, Mum A and I have a task to perform. Mum C, it's your turn to drink the truth and dare juice.

Mum C

Stats
Age: 29
Height: 152cm
Weight: 63 kilos. Mostly concentrated on my backside.
Number of kids: One remarkable two-year-old boy.
Number of husbands: One. Though this is subject to change.

I was at the supermarket a couple of months ago shivering in the refrigerator aisle, and while reaching for the standard bottle of low-fat milk with my standard block of boring mid-range cheese and the standard six-pack of low-fat yoghurt, my eyes slid over to the flavoured milk section. I snapped my eyes away, thinking piously of the skinny jeans at the back of my closet (where they have been lovingly stored, waiting for me, for two years now) but my eyes had a mind of their own and kept returning to the bottles with their Double Chocolate and Espresso and Iced Latte and Mocha Kenya contents, scanning quickly over them as if they were some forbidden lovers from a prior life. But something was different. Nestled between this naughty caffeine and sugar rush, was a little bottle of pale green milk. What a remarkable thing! How could I possibly resist further exploration?

I grinned from ear to ear as I dropped the bottle into my

shopping basket, snorted as I paid for it, giggled all the way home and cackled when I poured myself a small glass. I was swaying with excitement when I took a sniff and hooted as my face turned a similar shade to the contents of the glass. I took a hefty swig, slammed the glass down, made a noise that the Viking warriors of old would have identified with and screeched a bit more.

This is what my life has become. You see, motherhood has imposed on me far too much sense, and sensibility. They came along two years ago as I pushed out the placenta and took away with it all the frivolousness that I had been cultivating for 27 years. Frivolousness was replaced with guilt and the urge to cry during soapies. No longer can I justify spending a fortune on ridiculously uncomfortable boots. Instead, I spend a fortune on ridiculously expensive bits of plastic that make annoying noises, shrill crooning and overly-enthusiastic renditions of the alphabet that you simply cannot tune out. Worse, the damned songs are catchy and you find yourself singing them while you blunder bleary eyed to the bathroom at 4am. But that's only when the all-encompassing mummy guilt isn't coinciding with earth-guilt, which sees me spend a fortune on wooden toys and get confused ... did I just kill a tree for this little hammer and peg contraption?

Bizarre ethical dilemmas aside, where is the spark of life? Where are the thrills?

Amidst all this busy boredom I received a delicious invitation. 'Want to play?' it purred. It invited me to keep secrets from my husband, recapture myself, recreate myself, let it all hang out – yes, let those mummy rolls hang loose and free. Don't suck my gut in and let the bile pour forth.

Embrace my inner bitch and bitch about my ever-expanding innards.

How could anyone resist such a proposal?

You see, at the back of my mind I keep thinking that there has to be more to life than this. The thrill must exist outside of green milk. There's got to be more to life than a well-hidden Cadbury's Fruit & Nut bar, consumed while you stand at the open cupboard, careful not to crinkle the packaging lest anyone ask what you have there. That sweet tingle of naughtiness surely has to be found somewhere other than in scratching a mosquito bite when you've been told not to.

Oh, we all know that the two-year-old I have tearing around the place provides lots of entertainment as he destroys his father's treasured science fiction books. And yes, spending every day with him is just lovely. He is hilariously adorable with his new words and constantly astonishes me with how swiftly he catches on to new ideas. But amidst his entertaining, growing, loveliness, *I* am beginning to disappear.

I have a degree sitting in its dusty frame on the bookshelf and though I was wearing that silly little hat only a handful of years ago, I can barely remember the girl that graduated: young, keen, sleep deprived for all the right reasons, who was still harbouring rebellious tendencies and who was all set to travel, to get her PhD, to *do* stuff! I was going to tour Asia, do a teaching stint there, move to some strange and bizarre place (like Tasmania, for instance), maybe even get a dog! I knew I was unlikely to change the world, I was never going to join the UN or do any work in war torn countries, but I was going to be part of the world and have a bloody good time in it.

But now, where I used to read a pile of books a week for sheer pleasure, I now look at them in terms of time. How long would it take me to finish that book? How many nana naps does that work out at? While I am pondering these things, I wonder whether I would have time to sneak in a nap right now instead of pondering further. Maybe if I pop *Finding Nemo* on for the eighteenth time this week, I could sneak a nap in between the sharks and the turtles.

I spend my days clearing plastic off the floor while the boy deposits more plastic onto another bit of floor along with some half chewed lumps of vegemite sandwich. My hugely anticipated trips are no longer to some exotic beach destination or to some ancient ruins, but rather to Coles. I get excited over cleaning products. I squealed, actually *squealed*, when I saw a new scrub-free toilet cleaner. And the vibrant sex life of a 20-something-year-old woman has been packed away neatly along with those skinny jeans.

Early nights, my poor husband has had to learn, are for sleeping. Sex, if it happens, is scheduled in on a weekend so that I can sleep in. It's a payment of sorts.

A sex schedule? How can it get worse than that? you may ask. Well, I have recently begun contemplating watching American soapies. And if that wasn't bad enough, I have started knitting ...

It won't be long until I am lost forever and some strange Stepford wife sits in my place. Not a very good Stepford wife at that, because mummy-lobotomy or not, I doubt I will ever have the sparkling sink that the FlyLady's dedicated followers have. Goodness, this is further evidence of my fall that I know who and what the FlyLady is. Well, it's clear why I accepted Mum A's offer.

The cryptic email was swiftly replied to with a nonchalant 'Yeah, like, whatever. I don't really care.' Okay, it was actually 'YES PLEASE! WANNA WANNA WANNA! GIMME!' but the eagerness didn't seem to turn the other two mummies off and so we embarked on our strange journey. These virtual strangers were learning intimate things about me, had the power to manipulate my life for days, weeks, months at a time with the tiny little words 'truth' or 'dare' and I didn't care. The thought of it made me feel alive again, made me think beyond nappies and bath toys. These women would expose my soul not just to themselves, but also to me, I was hoping. But more than that, they wanted *me* to play with *them*. This wasn't about setting up a playdate with our children, this wasn't about being a mum, this wasn't about anything or anyone else other than me. Thinking that someone wanted to play with me again was altogether thrilling.

The anonymums had been silent for a while. I'd checked my emails every day, waiting for a mission, disappointed when there was none but also a little glad to be getting on with my comfortable old routine. By the end of the week, I thought that perhaps it had all fallen by the wayside, as so many mummy projects do and so I sighed wistfully and returned to the way things were. I worked on my degree, kept my son happy, slept when and where I could, dreamed impossible dreams of Roman adventures and Venetian exploits and just generally plodded along. Just as I was back to being dreadfully comfortable, I checked my secret account, just in case.

'In box has 1 new message.'

I sat with my mouth agape, looked around to make sure my husband was suitably occupied with a dirty nappy, and read on.

To: Mum C
From: Mum B
Subject: Dare

Dear one who has not revealed as much as some,

As Down There has been a hot topic for Some People (read: me) lately, it would be nice to see some Mum C action in that area. Find yourself a beautician who's waxed it all and ... wax it all off. C goes Copacabana.

Yours hairlessly,

B

I was mortified. I read it again in the vague hopes that it was daring me to go to Copacabana. Nope. Perhaps it was a dare to listen to some Barry Manilow? Nope. Well maybe I was thinking of the wrong thing. Surely my sisters in boredom couldn't mean what I thought they meant. But no, it was true – my sisters in boredom were every bit like real sisters: evil, cruel, mean hags. They wanted someone to pour wax on my pubes and rip the hairs out by the roots.

They wanted me not to bare my soul, but to bare it all (something far more painful).

Nope, not happening. There was no way I was doing it.

You have to understand that my fanny has been open to view by four people in my entire adult life: my husband who knocked me up and the two midwives and obstetrician that dealt with the consequences of being knocked up. That's it. No-one else. Not even me. The one time I even came close to having a peek was during labour when the midwife asked if I wanted a mirror to see what was happening down there. I told her that if they provided any such thing, I would simply stop pushing. There's a reason our eyes aren't on our knees – some things we are just not meant to see. And now they wanted me to bare it to some stranger brandishing hot wax? As they would say in Brazil, no way José!

I was annoyed. I was looking forward to this email. I wanted a dare, something good, something fun! I wanted to be asked to ... I don't know what, but not this! This was just too much, it was too hard! It was then that it occurred to me that I wanted a dare that was safe, one that wasn't truly a dare at all. I started down this truth and dare path because I was stuck in a mummy rut, because my brain, my attitude, my very essence were stagnating in routine blah-ness. I knew I needed to do something different, but when given this new idea to try, I dismissed it out of hand because it was uncomfortable. Okay, more than uncomfortable. Painful. Embarrassing. Humiliating.

Hard luck, chickadee. Time to drop those daks.

Resolving to stop being a cry-baby, I had a bit of a ponder. Was the point of the dare to be hairless or to have someone else do it? Settling on the idea that it was the ends and not the means, I waited until the little one's afternoon nap time before rummaging through my bathroom cabinet for a box of wax strips I had bought many moons ago in an effort to curb the foliage on my legs. After one strip, I had decided that I liked my legs hairy after all and put the box into the cupboard, forgotten until that moment.

I was determined to be strong and brave. I dropped my pants and read the instructions. Apparently it was not safe for genital areas but could be used for bikini lines, so, just to see what I would be in for, I drowned out the protests from my brain and slapped the strip on before I had a chance to change my mind.

I thought I was being courageous. I wasn't. I was being incredibly short sighted and really rather stupid because instead of changing my mind before the wax strip was on my pubes, I changed my mind when it was well and truly attached to them. I looked at the little white strip that seemed to grow as I stared at it in horror. What had I done? No, wait, I knew what I had done, but how the holy hell could I undo it? The box said that the wax wasn't water soluble. Disbelieving, I tried washing it off – it wasn't water soluble. I went into a panic, ploughing the depths of my mummy-brain for the inane advice I had received over the years. Mayonnaise works for chewing gum, doesn't it? Is that the same sort of thing? Or was that peanut butter and sunshine? I couldn't sit out on my balcony with peanut butter slathered over my groin! What would my neighbours think?

No longer relying on my brain to come up with a stellar solution, I accepted my fate and grabbed the end of the wax strip. One quick, confident pull was all it would take. It would be over in moments. I could do this; I'd pushed a baby out of my vagina. I could do this. This? Ha! It would be nothing! I am woman, hear me roar!

Or whimper, as the case turned out to be, while I painstakingly and painfully pulled at the wax strip, feeling each individual hair being ripped out by its root, the twanging almost audible in my tortured mind. My eyes stung, my nose ran and

I continued the laboured tugging of my pubic hair. It went on for what felt like days but finally the hair-riddled strip was in my hands. I looked down and inspected my work. I was lopsided. It was as if some butcher's paper was covering a quarter of a map of Tasmania. It looked wrong, so very wrong. It needed to be fixed but there was no way I was doing that to myself again, so I washed myself off and, when the little one was awake, we went for a walk around the shopping centre; I was looking for a place that could fix me while trying to seem terribly casual about it. For some reason, it was very important to me that I didn't appear to be a novice in the bald fanny brigade.

I found a beautician's shop, nicely secluded and in a quiet area of a quiet mall. I made an appointment for a 'full Brazilian', suppressing the terror that was threatening to leap into my voice at every turn.

The time of the appointment arrived far too quickly. As the time drew near, I realised that as much as I didn't want to be waving my fanny in a stranger's face, I was more dismayed about waving my flabby belly at them. Flabby people don't get waxes like this. It's something only taut, tanned, slim and gorgeous people do, which I wasn't. I felt I would be intruding, like turning up at the Playboy mansion puffy eyed, tired, flabby and short-arsed in ill-fitting jeans and t-shirt among the glamorous, bikini-clad bunnies.

What was the point of all this? I was never going to wear a bikini! Or go to Brazil for that matter!

I arrived at my appointment and pretended to read a trashy magazine while I waited; all the while my mind was yelling at me to get out of there, that I didn't belong, that they would just laugh at me when the waxer saw her waxee and then heard what I wanted.

Someone finally called my name. I got up and followed the reassuringly normal looking person (not a stick insect) into a small room and avoided her eyes when I told her what I wanted. She said 'sure' and asked me to take off my pants behind the curtain while she got on with preparing the wax. She didn't laugh at me. She didn't say anything at all, really. It was like my request was normal, ordinary, run of the mill.

Confused by this, I did as she asked and then lay down on the bed as instructed (which looked enough like a hospital bed to set me at ease about my lower nakedness). She then set to work.

The thing about having someone else ripping the hair from your fanny is that they don't really care. They aren't gentle or timid. They don't fear your pain. And because you are their customer and have asked that they perform the procedure (even paid good money for them to do so!), you are forced to suck it up. I'd be damned if I was going to show the pain and fear. And the pain ... the magnitude of pain! Oh dear God, the owieness of the pain. I drifted into what was possibly some form of shock as the pain seemed to recede on one side, numb almost. Blissful numbness. But then she attacked the other side. I scratched my eye to wipe away a tear without alerting the woman to my pain. I coughed a yelp. I bit my tongue. Eventually the numbness took over again.

And then suddenly she was done. The pain was gone, as was my hair. No lingering agony. I was left alone to get dressed. I looked down at myself and was reminded for the first time in over 15 years of the Barbie doll I played with as a child. I was bald, bizarrely bald. My underpants brushing against me felt strange. I felt different walking out of that place, confident, like I was part of the in-crowd. I spent most of that afternoon looking at other women, wondering what they had going on down there, wondering if they knew what I had – namely, nothing.

I felt inexplicably proud.

The confidence boost wasn't the only outcome from the experience. A rather more predictable outcome was my husband's interest in the area. And when I say interest, I mean, erm, you know, *interest*. Apparently the smoothness is appreciated, as nobody wants an unexpected dental flossing. His interest wasn't just in sex but in oral sex. Lots of it. And what I found intensely odd about all of this was that he wasn't doing it for reciprocated benefits. It was all about me, like he was rediscovering me, like I was new. He asked me what prompted such an odd move. My reply was simple – 'boredom'. I was surprised to see how readily he accepted that as a reason. Perhaps he'd been sensing my listlessness over the last couple of years after all.

It's an interesting feeling being bald. Ironically, although I have reverted to a pre-pubescent state in terms of looks down there, I feel more grown up. The feminist in me, having been backed into a corner already by my insistence on shaving my armpits, has thrown her hairy arms up in despair and doesn't know what to do. I at once love the feel of the lack of hair, the smoothness, the silkiness, but hate the message that women need to be smooth, hairless and perfect Barbie dolls to be attractive or even acceptable to society.

It's a moot point though, really. It was an interesting diversion from the norm, it broke me out of certain ruts and it made me feel different, but I think my membership in the Smooth Fanny Society is very temporary. Too much pain, not to mention the effort of getting a babysitter and trying not to reveal what the appointment was for; this was practically a dare in itself.

It will be fun while it lasts, but it made me wonder about what Mum A has in store for my truth. Amazing then, that when I open her email the following day, I find out that visiting the truth can be more painful than ripping your pubic hair from your body.

To: Mum C
From: Mum A
Subject: Truth

Ms C,

There must be days when you wish that you'd never had a child. (Shock! Gasp! Faint!) And I don't mean in a joking, appeal-to-the-heavens way, nope. I mean in that cold, hard, angry way, when you look at him and imagine the film star or even just the quiet life that could have been yours if he'd never been born. We've all been there but nobody talks about it. You will.

Ms A

It's one of those mummy secrets, a real one. One we dare not utter to anyone because as it is a real mummy secret, it's also mummy-circle suicide. People will turn away from you in disgust, hold their children away from you and suddenly find it too hard to meet your eyes as they pass around the packet of chocolate biscuits. They will whisper to each other and sniff haughtily at you. And while they are doing this, while you're feeling like the gum that they are scraping from their shoes with a wet-wipe to protect their perfectly manicured nails, you will know it's not because they are disgusted with you. More so, it's that they are afraid of confronting their own feelings. The secret that one feels and must never utter is that sometimes we wish we hadn't had our children.

In typical mummy-circle style, I feel I must start this truth gushing about how much I love my boy. Somebody once said that having a child is like having a piece of your heart walking around outside your body and, while I cringe at the sickly sweetness of the sentiment, I admit that she was onto something because that's how he feels to me. I feel all of his pains, choke up a little when some other rotten child won't play with him at the park, and am uplifted by his joy and laughter. The pride I feel when he meets every milestone makes my heart ache. And his absolute beauty, even as he's deftly unpacking all the shelves in Coles, is breathtaking. I often catch myself looking at him, astonished that he is mine, that I am his mother, that our worlds revolve around each other. In those moments before his sleepy eyes close at a ridiculous hour at night, there's nowhere I would rather be. All that soft, warm, comfortable, beautiful love is like nothing I have ever felt before.

And yet ...

Sometimes during those quiet moments I wonder where I would now be if I didn't have him. I would be living my planned life: university would be coming to an end, my passport would have a few exotic stamps, and I would have a disposable income that wasn't earmarked to pay for disposable nappies. I would be living somewhere bigger and, obviously, cleaner. And right about now, I would probably be thinking about trying to conceive a child. It might be just a passing fancy for a year or so while I carried on studying, working and travelling. I wonder what sort of mother I would have been given those extra years to mature and prepare myself for the role.

And yes, avert your eyes, dainty mothers, for there was a time when I wished with all my might that I had waited.

When he was a newborn, in those first shocking weeks of sleep deprivation and exploding boobs, when all the pregnancy happy hormones were long gone and ahead of me there was only dirty nappies, vomit and screaming, I thought it then. I never said it out loud, not properly. I even toned down my emotions when talking to my husband. I couldn't say 'I wish I hadn't had him', couldn't face the look that I knew a mother would receive at saying such a thing, so I said 'I can't do this'. When he offered all his support and told me how much he knew I could do it, all I wanted to do was lash out at him with something heavy and painful. How could he be so blasé about this? How could he not see? He clearly didn't understand what I was going through – but how could he? I wouldn't tell him. I skirted around it all the time: 'What have we done?' I'd ask, nervously laughing; and 'This was a bad idea!' while holding up a dirty nappy, inviting laughter at the situation; and 'I'm not cut out to be a mother' while I scrubbed poo off the amazing exploding-nappy boy. But only in secret, stolen moments, when everyone was asleep could I whisper, 'I wish that condom had bloody well worked' and then cry myself into a guilt-ridden sleep for 40 minutes until the baby woke again, screaming, wanting me, needing me, being attached to me.

What sort of mother, after all, wishes away their precious, glorious bundle of joy?

With guilt like that weighing us down, with this unspoken code of what is unspeakable hanging over our heads, is it really any wonder that many of us spiral down into the depths of Post Natal Depression? For the early months of my son's life, I was more or less housebound. I couldn't bear to travel any further than the local shops for fear that he would cry and that people would look at me and wonder why I was letting it happen, wonder what sort of mother I was. I knew that they'd see right through me, they'd see my dire secret, so I had to hide away. People were only allowed to see the loving, doting mother, confident and in control. No-one was allowed to see the lost, confused woman, wondering what on earth was going on in her life and where things went from here.

All through those months, my heart flip-flopped between a desperate, primal love for my son and a strange indifference. Not towards him but towards the whole motherhood gig. I wasn't enamoured of it. I didn't squeal with delight every time he burped, nor did I laugh at the cuteness of his fart. I didn't relish staying at home and watching *Dr Phil* every lunchtime. And I found *Oprah* positively nauseating. I fell deeper and deeper into myself, as I let my world become smaller. And, as I let that happen, I resented it. And, as I resented it, I blamed my son.

During that time, my husband said something about him wishing things were back to the way they used to be. I was furious with him. I was furious with the ease with which he could say something like that, how he didn't feel the torture that I felt inside. I was furious about how society made it okay and acceptable for men, generally the secondary caregiver to a child, to express themselves honestly about something so monumental, while women, the primary caregivers, had to keep it locked away, had to let it eat them up inside. I was furious with how he looked at me after he said that, wanting reassurance and *sympathy*, for goodness sake! Sympathy! From me!

And I was furious that I agreed with him. Things had been so much better before.

So I did the only thing I could do with all that fury: I sat on the floor and sobbed big, heaving, body-racking sobs. I wailed at my husband, asking him what was so [profanity] bad for him? He got to keep his [profanity] life! He got to go to [profanity] work and get [profanity] time [profanity] away from this [profanity] place. He wasn't the [profanity] one having to get up every [profanity] three hours at night for an hour at a time. And then he has the nerve to wish things different? How dare he?! Oh go [creative profanity involving himself and a farm animal]!

And he finally got it. He finally realised what had been going on under his nose for all those months and, while I still hadn't said it, he got it. And knowing that someone else knew at once terrified me (what if they take my baby away?) and liberated me. Finally, someone could help me. Someone that I loved and who loved me now knew the deepest darkest secret in my heart and he stuck by me and helped me.

Time passed. My husband took on more responsibility. He got up with me during the night feeds, just for the companionship. He would change the nappy while I arranged the mountain of pillows that were needed to breastfeed our son. He took on more of the household chores, so that I could take a nap when our son slept instead of putting on loads of washing. He got up with our boy on weekend mornings to let me catch up on as much sleep as I could. He insisted that we went out for breakfast sometimes, and that we go out to a park or a festival or a show.

He slowly brought me back to myself.

Soon enough, I felt like the old me. I was eager to be in company, eager to learn, happy to move away from my comfort zone on the couch. I was me ... plus one.

I no longer wish my son away. But I do still wonder. I still wonder what life would have been like if he wasn't here. I still sigh wistfully while refusing research positions at overseas universities. I fall into daydreams about what might have happened if I had gone to Holland as I had planned before that fateful second line popped up on the pregnancy test. As I run through the campus at lightning speed, I envy those sitting around, drinking leisurely cups of coffee, planning their latest arts projects.

But then I get home and see the way my boy's face lights up as I walk through the door. I hear the giggles, the 'mummy, mummy, mummy', the gibberish tales of his time spent with his dad, and there's nowhere I would rather be.

It's hard to find the words when talking about this truth. I've told very few people my feelings because it is such a taboo subject. You just know that they will watch you with an eagle eye, see every instance of cranky mummy and turn it into something more sinister.

I have known for a long time that this was a big truth in my life. I knew that it was a truth that I would hide when I could but would share where it could benefit others. There are many women out there who suffer PND and regret having their babies. There are many other women who don't suffer PND but are in poor circumstances and thus regret having their babies. I suppose it's all about realising and accepting that we were women, independent women with our own minds, our own hearts, our own dreams and our own lives for many, many years before we became mothers. Regretting losing some (and often a large amount) of that is hard to deal with. Especially so when you lose it all suddenly. Nine months is all there is between you and not only a radical life change but also a radical personality change.

*

A real-life anonymums meeting looms on the horizon. It's been a month since our last, online, one and now it's time to don the trench coat and the hat and set off, keeping to the shadows and slinking into the night. Or at least into Mum A's Sydney hotel room. Between my hairlessness and oft-wished childlessness, Mum B's fantasies and Mum A's mother-bashing, we may spend the whole time staring at the floor, blushing furiously.

the second meeting

'Mum A?' the voice over the intercom asked hesitantly.

It took me a split second to remember that we were one and the same. I pressed the buzzer. 'Come on up! Twelfth floor. I'm directly in front of the lift in room 1206.'

The pair of them were at my door faster than I could compose myself. There was no time for a dash of lip-gloss, or hair fixing, or shirt pulling down. It would just be me ... and them.

Which was how it should be, I suppose.

'It's so quiet ...' Mum B said, as the three of us stood in the doorway to the studio apartment I was staying in for the next two nights.

'Eerily so,' Mum C agreed as we headed inside and she started looking around the room suspiciously. 'You know, I'm sort of waiting for children to ambush us with open vegemite sandwiches and spray us with chocolate milk.'

I was used to the silence by now. It always hit me in the same way, though. Every single time, post-kids, I'd entered a hotel room by myself, I'd simply sit on the bed, bags still packed, and revel in the silence.

But it wasn't the silence that had me standing stock-still

now. Rather, it was catching sight of the three of us in the mirror that ran the length of the short hallway.

Could the three of us be any more different? No, we couldn't. But the weird thing was, for all our differences, we also went together in an odd sort of way. Small, medium and large – Mum C was tiny, I had the exact 'average Australian woman' measurements and Mum B towered over us both, even without heels. Early, mid and late 30s – Mum C was 29, I was 34 and Mum B was heading towards 40. Espresso, chai and hot white chocolate – Mum C was dark, I was your standard Caucasian and Mum B was best kept off the beach.

I clapped my hands together to break the silence. 'Right, then. Espresso, chai, or hot white chocolate?' Bugger, did I just say that out loud?

The pair of them gave me an odd look. 'Coffee, thanks,' they said in unison.

When the coffee was made and I'd stopped checking us all out, we went and perched in the living room, none of us knowing what to say next. I'm guessing they were probably thinking something along the same lines as I was, that this was altogether too much like internet dating. We'd gotten on so well online, but now, IRL ...

'So is this what it's like to be a famous author?' Mum B asked me, looking around the apartment.

I almost spat out my hot beverage. 'I wouldn't know,' I told her, after I'd recovered. 'I don't know any famous authors. But if you're talking about me, I'm sorry to say I'm not really one. It's more one per cent nice, silent hotel rooms and 99 per cent writing a few words in between dropping off and picking up the kids and standing about in the supermarket wondering if it's too slatternly to have sausages and mash three nights of the week.' Amazingly, I was in Sydney care of a TV doco. series being shot on the topic of motherhood. I was going to be interviewed as an 'expert'. If only they knew the truth about the sausages ...

'Oh,' Mum B replied. 'I was kind of hoping for feather boas and champagne on tap.'

'Sometimes my publicist gives me cab vouchers,' I told her, hoping to bolster her spirits a little.

'We might need one of those after we go out tonight,' Mum C cackled, and both Mum B and I shot each other the same look at the same time.

'She really does cackle!' Mum B laughed, which set me off as well. Mum C had written about cackling over her lime green milk. But that someone so tiny could cackle like that ...

That one cackle was all we needed to get started.

We couldn't shut up after that.

*

By the time we'd had two drinks each at the ivy bar (note that we're still cool enough to go places that use lower case), we couldn't be fagged to get up from our spots on the low couches, so we stayed put and ordered from the bar menu. We were now drunk enough to talk about all we'd been through.

I polished off my drink before I got started. 'You know, Mum C, when I read your Santa dare ... I'm ashamed to say I was disappointed.'

'Disappointed?' Mum C replaced her drink on the coffee table in front of us. 'What were you expecting?'

'I don't know,' I shrugged. 'That I'd have to jump out of a plane?' I turned to Mum B before she could say anything. 'Yes,

yes. No jumping out of planes. But you know what I mean. When you suggested Santa, I just thought it would be too easy. But it wasn't. In the end, it was exactly the same kind of sky diving adrenalin rush. I think I've become so accustomed to not doing anything silly or different. Doing something even slightly outside of the norm is enough to set my heart a-racing now. How sad is that?'

'It's not sad,' Mum B told me. 'It's normal. Just be thankful you caught it early.'

I laughed. 'Sure. I mean, imagine if I'd gone ten years down the track and then, one day, bought Peach Trix instead of Lemon, on a whim. With no prior experience in excitement, my heart wouldn't be able to take it.'

Mum C shook her head at me. 'A good wife would only buy Sunlight, you know.'

'Huh. Maybe there's hope for me then. I'm too much of a cheapskate to buy Sunlight, even on special. You know something else I realised during the Santa dare?'

'What's that?' Mum B looked around for our waitress. 'A mother could starve to death in this place. Don't they know I'm used to eating at six o'clock and bedtime is nine thirty? Sorry, what were you saying?' She turned back.

'Oh, just that I think I use my kids as a barrier. No-one looks at me when I have two kids in tow. Not having them when I was doing the Santa thing ... it's threatening to line up and have people stare at you. I'd forgotten what it's like to have people scrutinise you, question you, look at you to see what you're up to – if you're a threat to them or their kids.'

'Ummm.' Mum B leaned forward slightly. 'Explain?'

I tried to gather my gin-sodden brain cells together. 'Okay, I know. I used to get it when I'd walk my son to day-care in his stroller. I had to walk alongside a main road for some way before I'd drop him off. I'd leave the stroller at the day-care centre and then walk home.'

'And?' Mum C urged me on.

'Well, the weird thing was, no-one would even glance at me on the walk there, but on the way home, people driving by would look. Not in an, "Oh my God, she's so hot" way, but they'd just notice me. That I was there ... a person ... a woman ... walking.'

Mum B now sat back in her armchair. 'Ah, right. Now I get you. The Invisible Cloak of Motherhood?'

I nodded. 'That's it. That walk back was really freeing, too. I only noticed after my son changed centres that I'm rarely ever out and about just being me. I'm either with the kids, or at home, working. I think that needs to change, because I've caught myself a few times recently thinking I'm excluded from society.'

'How so?' Mum B asked me.

'Okay, the other night, I was watching a doco. about Paris on TV. There were people sitting, drinking coffee at the sidewalk cafés, other people strolling past, just ... being alive. And I watched them like they were aliens. I kept thinking, "Wow, some people are allowed out". You know, just the thought of that was completely alien to me.'

Mum C sighed. 'Oh, yes. I know that feeling.'

Mum B nodded. 'Me too.'

'It's the tethering thing that really gets me, I think,' I continued. 'I mean, I'm allowed out, but I'm always tethered. Being allowed out means making sure my husband or parents are watching the kids. And if I go out while they're at day-care and kindy, I feel guilty. Because while they're in care, I should be working. Because having your kids in care means you're a bad, selfish, evil mother, doesn't it?' I shook my head, knowing this wasn't true, but it was true to how I felt, which was enough.

'I know my husband doesn't get this amazing "allowed out" coffee-swilling-time-in-Paris feeling, but it's different for him because when he goes to work, he's not tethered. The kids aren't his problem. I think what I'm looking for is just a bit of time where I'm simply me, with only me to think about. Which brings me back around to the "selfish" bit again, because good mums don't think that, or want that, do they?'

Mum B laughed. 'No, they love nothing more than being at home with their kids. And the gin and valium bottles.'

'I know I do,' Mum C chimed in.

I shook my head again. 'Mother guilt is a bitch. I'm going to try something out, though. Next week, I'm going to drop the kids at day-care and kindy, and stop for a half-hour coffee and read the paper. Baby steps.'

'Sounds good.' Mum B nodded.

'But enough about me. Tell me about your truth.' I raised an eyebrow at Mum B. 'And your dare.' I looked down at Mum C's skirt.

'I can't believe you're still talking to me now that you know what goes on in my head,' Mum B groaned.

I couldn't help but crack up. 'I'll be avoiding dinner parties at your house because of your wandering thoughts over your famous *Coq au vin*.'

'Well, you did ask. And I did point out I don't actually imagine people I know doing it.'

'Did it change your life?' Mum C brought us back on track.

Mum B thought about Mum C's question for a second or two before answering. 'I have to say it was what Dr Phil would call a really good exercise. It's been a long time since I had any space in my brain to consider what turns me on. I really had started to think it was all rushing through the sex to get to the main event – sleep. At least I'm thinking about sex in a friendly way again – rather than adding it to the weekly To Do list.'

'So you're refreshed in a sexual way.' Mum C tilted her head to one side. 'Interesting.'

'It helped to remind me that sex is actually fun ...' Mum B paused on seeing our expressions. 'No, really. It's just that you need to make time, not just shove it onto the end of a crappy day. I saw a story by a sexpert once who advised making actual appointments for it. I don't know that I'd go that far, but I'm open to thinking about it more often.'

Unlike Mum C, who didn't look at all impressed with this idea, I was willing to entertain it for a moment. 'Appointments ...' I considered the idea. 'I haven't heard of that one before. It makes sense, though. I mean, the rest of my life runs to a precise schedule. Why not sex, too?'

Mum B shrugged. 'Why not? Though I'd bet on Mum C getting more than her fair share, lately.'

The pair of us turned on poor Mum C now with evil grins.

Mum C shivered slightly under our vulture-like gazes. 'I'm still having flashbacks to the searing pain. But, yes, like I said in my dare write-up, there was serious interest. Less so now I have re-growth. I can see he's too scared to ask if I'm getting it re-done or not. He's heard my feminist rants before on perverted men who like the pre-pubescent look.'

'But you said you liked it ...' I continued my line of questioning.

'I did.' Mum C nodded. 'Which I was surprised about.

I think it was the novelty of something different and a bit daring, more than anything. I didn't like it enough to go back and get it done again, though. If I could manage the mind-numbing itchiness when re-growth occurs, shaving might have been a possibility but nah, bugger that. A good trim every now and then does me just fine.'

'It sounds a lot like my lippie dare, you know,' Mum B mused. 'I enjoyed the change, and my husband did too, but I wouldn't want to do it all the time.'

My eyes widened. 'I thought that lipstick dare was *huge*. I honestly couldn't believe no-one in your family commented. That they just let it slide! Surely it must make you wonder what else you could get away with?'

Mum B paused for a second. 'You know what it made me realise? That people don't notice half as much about us as we think they do. We waste so much of our lives wondering what other people think, or what they might say. It's just a restriction we put on ourselves. There's a lot of freedom in the idea that nobody really gives a hoot about whether I wear red lips or a red nose.'

With this, our mezze dips and olives came and we fell upon them.

After a good sustaining mouthful, I turned my attention back to Mum C. 'And your truth?'

Mum C froze, Turkish bread in hand. 'I'm still embarrassed about the truth. I hope you don't think my son is ... unwanted.'

I shook my head. 'Of course not – unplanned and unwanted are two very different things,' I said after spitting out an olive pip.

'As is unloved,' Mum B added. 'And he sounds like one very loved little boy.'

Mum C nodded. 'It's funny you should mention the semantics of the whole thing because you'd be amazed how many words I've used to not say the big ones. He was a surprise, he was unexpected, he was a bit of a shock, he was a change in my plans ... God forbid I should ever say he was an accident. Or that I should ever think he was a *mistake*.'

I knew exactly what she was talking about. 'We hide behind our words a lot, don't we? Women, I mean. I couldn't count how many times I've called a child "spirited" when what I actually meant was "little shit".'

'It's because we have to maintain this illusion of perfection.'

Mum C polished off her hummousy bread. 'Which is exactly what leads to our downfall. Motherhood is a job and no matter how great your job may be, it isn't great all the time. At the office, when the girl in the next cubicle is chewing your ear off about her insipid love life or the boss is giving you strife about a deadline ... it's okay to whinge about that. But mothers whingeing about motherhood just isn't allowed. You wanted kids, now you deal with it. In silence. My husband was just as much to blame for our ... umm ... surprise. I know he and his workmates bitch about fatherhood all the time, but us? Nope. Not allowed. Don't even *think* it, let alone say it.'

Mum B nodded as she listened. 'It scares people. There's a code of silence around motherhood. I've always thought it's weird how we seem to want to shield the reality of the job from other women.'

'That was exactly where I went wrong,' Mum C agreed. 'I put my mummy mask on before I set foot outside the door each morning. Everyone thought I was doing so well. And of course, then I was too terrified to tell them how absolutely appallingly I was actually doing. This was my job, and it was such a supremely important job. Failing to be a good accountant is one thing, failing to be a good mother is in a completely different order of magnitude.'

'So no-one knew how you felt?' Mum B asked.

'There were a couple of people who I talked to about it online, people who had been through PND and who understood. The internet is great for that – there's fantastic support out there. Anyway, it's amazing to be able to be truthful about it in real life as well. I've come to terms with my feelings, though. I don't share them willy-nilly, but I feel it's my duty to open up if it might help some other new mum feel less like a monster. Even so, even though I'm mostly secure in my knowledge that I really am not a monster, that I'm really not a bad mother, I still had a slightly panicked reaction when I read that "worst mother" truth. I was terrified that it would be me – not literally me, of course, but someone like me.'

I placed my drink back on the table. 'I've got to admit I was a bit worried about my "worst mother" truth as well. Mother judging is supposed to be the antithesis of what we're about, right?'

'But that was the point, wasn't it?' Mum B said. 'You looked behind the judgment to find out what was really going on. You could have just written her off.'

I started to reach for the mezze plate, but then pulled my hand back. I didn't deserve any more baba ghanoush. 'I think I did write her off for a bit.'

'No, be fair. She sounds a bit ... full-on.' Mum C's eyes widened. 'People who dump all of their emotional baggage on you after five minutes can freak anyone out.'

Mum B laughed. 'Like us.'

Mum C grinned. 'Yes, but in that case, it's okay, because we asked for it to be heaped on top of us. Now.' She turned to me. 'Finish that baba ghanoush so we can go and eat something substantial.'

'Okay,' I agreed. 'But you only get dessert if you promise to start working hard on your Big Dares.'

January

January

Mum A

How could we be back to torturing me so quickly? I guess a month passes much more quickly during the Christmas madness, when the list in your head extends to five pages, rather than your usual two, and the only present you don't have to shop for is your own (and even then, you need to remember to throw out really good hints unless you want an oh-so-festive foot spa).

I truly didn't think it could happen so fast, but things have actually been slightly different around here since my first truth and dare. To be fair, I don't think it was so much the truth and dare, but our night out and some of the things I ended up admitting to. Talking about some of those feelings that have been cropping up scared me slightly. It was time to make some changes to my daily routine.

I started by taking that tiny step of having coffee at my favourite café on the way home from the kindy/day-care drop-off I did three days per week. The first day, I almost didn't stop. The excuses came all too readily: 'I have to collect that parcel from the post office that's been sitting there for four days now'; 'I must stop at the vet's and buy some more flea treatment for the cats'; 'I need to get home and hang the washing out'. It was the reminding myself about hanging the washing out that did it. Was I really so guilt-ridden I'd rather run home and peg out sheets than spend half an hour with myself? So I stopped.

The next day it was easier.

By the following week, it had almost become a habit. And three days per week was a goodly amount. Not too little, not too often; something I could look forward to, but not too much of a commitment. And if I had to skip a day here and there, I wouldn't feel too bad about it.

While I needed that second coffee in the morning, I found it was more than the caffeine that pepped me up. It was almost thrilling how people treated me when I was out by myself ... like an honest to God human being. Not that they didn't when I had kids with me, but when I was alone, they treated me like I was this amazing, independent creature who could pause for a second to decide exactly what she wanted (a flat white, thanks). This was opposed to the frazzled person they'd met before who belted out the first coffee order that came to mind because her thoughts were being overridden by little people screeching like banshees for dottie bikkies, babycinos and juice. It was also lovely to be a woman with a handbag for half an hour, rather than a mule lugging around a gigantic nappy bag. During my half-hour, I would read the paper pretty much in its entirety. I began to feel a bit less guilty about doing this; after all, I do write for the paper from time to time and really should be reading it on a daily basis. It was nice to catch up with the world that I remembered once existed beyond the 4WD window. Funnily enough, it was still there.

This one small change (some might say 'insignificant' change, but they would probably be male and allowed out every day, so it wouldn't count) made me want to make other small changes. So I started to question other things in my life. Not the big things, like 'Should we go and work overseas before it's too late?', 'Should we have that third baby?', 'Will I ever get the time to shave my legs again?' But the little things I could actually change. And one of the first things that came up was lunch.

For months now, I'd been coming home after a morning out with the kids at the gym, the park, or at a friend's house and giving them a sandwich with some fruit for lunch. Because it's a busy part of the day – making lunch/getting the kids ready for nap-time/tidying the house/doing the washing/unloading the dishwasher/making kindy and day-care lunches for the next day – I was finding I was eating the following for lunch every single day ...

A peanut butter sandwich and a chocolate milk.

Well, yum, yum, yum.

At 34, it was just a bit ... embarrassing, really. But it was too hard to think of anything else. And, even if I had, it would have been even harder to make it.

I knew one thing, though, I didn't want that sandwich and milk for lunch. I wanted a big girl lunch. I also knew I needed to start eating more vegetables and stop popping a multivitamin each day and crossing my fingers. But whatever I was going to make, it had to be easy. As easy as the lunch I was already having. Not long after making the decision to change, I came across a recipe being shared around on the mothers' forum I frequent. I changed it a bit (okay, a lot, I soak lentils for no man, or even for myself) and added a few items.

The following weekend, I made the recipe, cooked some rice up in the rice cooker and then made up eight meals in plastic containers and threw them into the freezer. Then I took one out each night, popped it in the fridge and ... whammo, there was lunch waiting to be nuked the next day.

Fancy a bite to eat?

> Mum A's lunch
>
> olive oil
> 2 medium brown onions, diced
> 2 medium-sized sweet potatoes, diced
> ½ large pumpkin, diced
> can of brown lentils, drained
> bottle of passata
> 2 teaspoons cumin
> 1 teaspoon turmeric
>
> Fry the onion in the olive oil and spices for a few minutes. Stir in the rest of the ingredients, cover and simmer until veggies are cooked through. Serve with rice, and eat peanut butter sandwiches and chocolate milk no more.

After a week of veggie curry for lunch, I have to admit my bowels and I were more than ready for a change. But I'm not willing to change back to eating kiddie-style, that's for sure. Oh, no. So, I've put the rest of the curry into the freezer for another time, and this week I'm moving on to cheese platters (refined, no?). I'm doing the whole bit – lavosh crackers, a spot of aged cheddar, a whisper of double brie, some nuts, a bit of dried fruit, some quince paste. Yesterday, I took my lunch box of cheesy delights to kindy where I was rostered on for the day and got laughed at by two mothers and the kindy teacher. Must remember that conventional sandwiches are *de rigueur* in certain situations. Kindy is probably one of them.

Besides this, I've been trying out some other stuff as well. Over the holidays, my kids have been more than a tad obsessed with Grandma and Grandpa's pool. Often, it will be the first thing my son says as he scrambles up to standing in his cot each morning ... 'Grandma's swim?' But with the holiday season comes stuff: planning stuff, shopping stuff, wrapping stuff, decorating stuff and cooking stuff. And the pool takes time: packing time, driving time, dressing time, sun-screening time and swimming time. There have been more than just a few days when, badgered to go to the pool for the 500th time, I have snapped and taken the 'all the stuff we've got to do today' line and shoved another DVD on. But the other day, they kept badgering, so I took them, and realised just how their little faces light up in the pool. They love it so much and talk about it all the way home ... until, hungry with all the exercise, they start hassling for dinner. It wears them out nicely for the evening too, so early to bed for them and more time for me. The lesson? I've really got to let go and do more ... stuff. Too often I take the 'it's just too hard' road and choose the easier route. But this tends to bite me on the backside, because the 'it's just too hard' route always seems to be the less scenic one; it's boring. I might get stuff done, but only through sending small people to the naughty corner every five minutes.

So, yep, more stuff it will be – cheesy, chloriney or otherwise.

Disclaimer: just don't ask me to go camping. Like Mum B and her jumping out of planes thing, I have some limits.

Camping is not going to happen while the Club Meds of this world remain open for business.

I was so busy making my little changes, I almost forgot to get cracking on the big one. My Big Dare. But then a few things happened between my husband and me, and I got to thinking ... and reading ... and writing down some notes. It should be interesting.

I also almost forgot to watch out for Mum B and Mum C's emails that would contain my truth and dare. I say 'almost' because this means I only checked my secret email account maybe twice a day. This time around I wasn't quite so knee-knockingly scared. Still, when the truth came in, it wasn't what I was expecting. But, this time, I embraced the unexpected. After all, I was starting to see that the unexpected was precisely what I needed right now.

To: Mum A
From: Mum B
Subject: Dare

A,

This may seem like an easy dare at first as it's all in your head, but I've tried it at home and it gets complicated rather quickly. Your dare is to imagine an affair. Not in an 'oh, I wouldn't mind a bit of him' way, but to really take the time and think it out. Who, in your immediate circle, would you have an affair with? How would you set about doing it? What

> would it really be like? How would you see him? Hide what was going on? We're not talking about the 'I reserve the right to sleep with Hugh Jackman' stuff, but the real thing here.
>
> B

I was nattering away to one of my girlfriends at the gym the other day when my husband's personal trainer walked past. The two of us watched him walk by (being the approximate size of the Incredible Hulk, you couldn't really miss him). 'Does he look even larger than usual?' my friend asked me, squinting at him and pausing mid-conversation. And then, as this was much more interesting than what we'd been previously talking about, we switched topics. She mentioned how she knew a couple of women who'd slept with guys like this just to see what it felt like. She then asked me if I'd ever been interested in doing the same. The short answer: yuck, no. I'd always thought the gym guys were hideous. Too much muscle, poncing about with their protein power shakes in their little sippy cups. Bleh. She agreed – she'd never been interested in the muscle-man thing either and just didn't see the attraction. We both admitted we'd been more than a little shocked on hearing a number of our friends had partaken. I didn't think any less of them for it, but I was surprised so many women seemed to be into that kind of thing, because the web-necked football player-type was never going to do it for me.

So when Mum B truthed me to make up my own little secret affair, I knew it was never going to be one of those gym-boy fantasies. It was going to be more of an emotional connection. When I thought about even the tiniest connection I'd had over the past few years that I could possibly bring to the fore and fantasise about, one person stood out in my mind. He'd do. It could even be fun. I'd never be able to look at him at my husband's work Christmas party again without blushing and remembering what had gone on in my head, but maybe that would be fun too (especially after three G&Ts).

This guy is the exact opposite of the gym boys. He's not much taller than me (and I'm certainly not tall), and he isn't exactly a looker. He has more a pleasantish, kindish sort of face. I don't really know him all that well, but this is probably a good thing, because then he's more pliable, like Playdough straight out of the tub. He's not one of my husband's immediate workmates, but someone he works with from time to time, and someone I only see occasionally at his work functions. So why the interest in this shortish, pleasantish, kindish guy, who's starting to sound more like a Smurf than affair material? Well, I think it's mostly because he's one of the few men I've ever met who has actually asked intelligent questions about my job and then listened to my answers and *then* asked another intelligent question in return. Unheard of, really. Whenever I speak to him, we click. I enjoy talking to him at parties and kind of look forward to seeing him, maybe even wonder if he'll be there when my husband tells me there's a work function we need to attend together. He's funny, and nice.

Okay. I've really got to get away from the 'nice' bit.

The 'nice' bit keeps giving me pause. Because that's the thing: I can't have an affair with this guy; he's too nice! He has a wife, who's also nice. And kids who are probably nice as well.

But, wait. Wait. That's the whole point of this, isn't it? I'm being nice too. I'm not really doing this, it's all in my head. So, it's all okay. It'll be a nice affair. Hang on, can you have a nice affair? Or do they have to be all hot and heavy and clandestine and lustful? I guess not. I guess you could go either way. I can't see why you couldn't have a sweet little affair where no-one gets hurt. What was that old Alan Alda movie called? *Same Time Next Year*, I think. He and another woman meet, have a one-night fling then decide to meet up in the same way each year. No-one gets hurt. Everyone's happy. If you can skip over the fact they're miserable in their real relationships. But I guess it goes to show that affairs don't have to be all nasty, bunny boiling numbers. God, listen to me yakkity yakking.

Stalling now. Really stalling.

Right, so how to go about this affair of ours, then? I have no idea what sort of car he drives, or where he lives, or anything like that. I've just had a look and he's not on Facebook, and he's not in the phone book either, so I guess the first step would be to see if I could get his mobile or home phone number or address from my husband somehow. But then what would I do with it? No, scrap that. I'm hardly going to send him some sexy text out of the blue, or turn up at his home like a stalker. Which, I suppose, leaves me with two choices: I could make an appointment to see him at work (where he has his own office, with a door and all – I know this because I've been inside not once, but twice, to visit him in an official, non-affair, work-like capacity! I did have two kids under five with me both times, but still …); or I could wait for the yearly Christmas party and seduce him there.

Pause.

Vomit.

Let me add that I am definitely not the seductive type. If I imagine me trying to be seductive, the picture isn't pretty. In fact, he would probably think I was drunk, or joking, or both. No, I'm more ... dinner party-ish. So maybe that would be a better solution? Have him (and his family? Oh, foul thought ...) over for dinner. And then what? Seduce him in the laundry next to the cat food? If I do that, I must remember to remind him not to bang his head on the dryer. Honestly, I have no idea how people have affairs if it's this cringingly hard.

In fact, I have to admit I don't really get the affair thing at all. Maybe this is a good thing. Maybe it means I'm happy in my relationship – or I would be if I could only get my husband to put the washing-up detergent in the sink *before* he fills it with water, rather than at the end when it sinks to the bottom and sits there uselessly ... Sorry, where was I? Maybe it means I'm not looking elsewhere, and not having little seduction daydreams in my head, or wondering who I'm going to run off with next. Maybe it's because no-one would 'kiss' me if I listed myself on RSVP ... eek. Hadn't thought of that one before. Might skip over that.

Anyway, there are two things I don't get about affairs: first is the time factor, and second is how the least likely people seem to have them. Now, I don't know about the other anonymums, but I know (or think I know) where my husband is pretty much 100 per cent of the time. He's always contactable on his mobile. His roster is written up on the calendar, which, if I want to, I can check against the roster on his computer, which I can check against his pay slip. I control the money, so I get all the bills and check to see if the mobile calls all look okay, that the credit card statements look okay and so on. If he was suddenly going to have an affair, I think I'd notice. Sure, there are times he could 'slip' away. He's often on call overnight (could fit some booty call in instead, I suppose). And just last weekend, he went on a course for a whole Saturday. I knew where it was, though, so if I'd been suspicious, I could have checked up on him. As it was, he came home at midday anyway because it was boring (he hung out for the free lunch before bailing out, of course ...). I, however, could get away with much, much more if I wanted to. But this would mean cutting back on eBay and Twitter when I'm supposed to be working, and if I had to choose between sex and eBay, well ... eBay wins hands down every time, doesn't it? Who wants to have undetected sex when you can have undetected shopping instead?

The people-least-likely thing led me to think about when a girlfriend's father was outed as a long-time philanderer. It was a rude shock, because he is not a handsome man in the slightest. Rather, he is very large and very red in the face. He didn't even have the power thing going on. In fact, he wasn't very successful at all. He'd been having affairs for years, apparently, with several different women. He and his wife (my friend's mother) split up and then, after some time, he begged to be allowed to come back. She took him back. They bought a new home together. He cheated again with two different women, if I remember correctly (he's a hard man to keep up with, so I may be wrong on that account). They split up for good. He's now remarried and my friend has cause to believe he's cheating again. And he hasn't got any more handsome or more powerful, either. We've spoken about this at length over the years, the two of us, and she believes he cheats because he's insecure. Because he has so little self-worth that any interest he gets, he can't say no to. And maybe this is part of why something inside me recoils at the very idea of an affair. Because, to me, it means that, in part, you're not strong and emotionally secure. And it means you're not brave enough to step away from the unhappy situation you're in. You'd rather sneak around and lie than be truthful with yourself and move on.

I guess this is just me, though. Maybe I'm simply Ms Monogamy. Maybe it's because I'm pretty sure I have a reasonably low sex drive and always have. Maybe I just really love eBay. Who knows?

Or, um, maybe it's something else.

If I peel away the layers like an onion, I come to the true heart of the matter. Having an affair hurts. How do I know? Well ...

(Pause for a deep breath here before I let the truth out ...)

Because my husband almost had one once, before we were married. That is, he wanted to have an affair, but the problem was, she didn't. Despite not being in a relationship, she wasn't willing.

Another deep breath, just to keep me going. Just to stop the voices in my head that are now screeching, 'Don't want to think about it! Don't want to think about it!'

We still see this woman once in a while. I can see that my husband isn't at all interested in her like that anymore, but I find I'm always on the back foot with her. I don't know how to act when I'm around her. Do I say something about it? But that would be just a tad weird, wouldn't it? Years on? Or is it more embarrassing to be the little clueless wifey who knows nothing? I don't know ... And then there's always that nagging little voice – what if she *had* been interested? Would she be in my place now? With two kids? In my house? God knows, the

January

kids would probably look exactly the same because I didn't get a genetic look-in.

She's been away for a while, working overseas, but soon she'll be back, working with my husband again. I actually don't feel too worried about this. It's the past that concerns me, which seems odd. The old flame is coming back onto the scene and I'm worried about the past. It doesn't really make sense, but it's how it is – I'm more concerned with what might have been than where things could go from here. I suppose it's because we're different people now. When I look back, the thing was that neither of us were particularly happy with our lives at the time this all happened, which led to us not being particularly happy with each other, which led him to the affair that didn't happen. And while we obviously still have our issues, I think we're very careful now to pick up on early signs of unhappiness and to do something about it before it leads to ... someone else.

So, no. He didn't have an affair. But you know something ...? My heart doesn't care about that at all. He may as well have.

And this is probably why I'm not even keen on affairs in my head. Because I know firsthand that even the ones that don't happen can hurt like hell, years and years afterwards. Not to mention they cause all kinds of problems with trust and with doubt. This non-event manages to make a starring appearance in every big argument we have. The thing is, in his head it's something that never happened. But in mine, it's something that might have happened, except for her lack of interest, or might have happened but he's lying (I don't think so, but there's always a smidgin of doubt, isn't there?), or it's something that might happen next year (once an almost-cheater ...), or five years from now, or ... well, sometimes it's not good to have a writer's vivid imagination.

But back to the task at hand.

Focus, focus.

Just do it, as they say.

But I can't. I can't imagine this affair. This on-going, lie-producing, sneakily sneaking, ever-growing creature that would be a third person in our bed. (Fine, *sixth* person considering 'our bed' consists of the two of us, one five-year-old and two cats most nights. And it'd be *seven* if our youngest could break free from his cot.) Just the thought of having an affair gives me pains in my chest that I don't think are from the third coffee I shouldn't have had today. So, what I'm going to do is get rid of the 'affair' word and imagine a titillating fling instead. Just a little one-off. So quick and sudden that, even if it did happen you'd be questioning whether it was just a dream five minutes afterwards. As it is, even this makes my heart skip little beats again. And not in a pleasant way.

Okay, time to get on with it.

I'll begin with the office option. What I'll do is make an appointment to see him at his office. I'll arrive a few minutes late so I don't have to endure a torturous wait reading *New Idea* from 1995 in the waiting room, and then, when I'm called in, I won't dilly dally. Before he can object, or his secretary can walk in, or even before he can (please, no) be 'nice', I'll simply let him close the door behind us, push him up against it and let him have it. I'll avert my eyes from the pics of his wife and kids, and busy myself stripping him of his really not very professional moleskin jeans and RMs and then, when I've done that, I'll … give him some decorating advice.

See? I just can't do it. I don't have it in me to have an affair. And, anyway, giving him a makeover and refreshing his interior space (does that sound kinky or what?) would be so much more satisfying than an affair. (He and a much older guy share office space that was obviously furbished by the older guy in 1970 and has since been left quite, quite untouched, including the wood panelling and magazines ...)

And then, when he was close to naked? Well, I'd enjoy myself thoroughly re-dressing him in something slightly more fashionable. (Sweetheart, at the very least, walk into Country Road and the girls there will outfit you each season. Moleskins and RMs are for farmers, not for guys who work in premium office space in the middle of the CBD.)

Done with him, I'd hold one finger up to my lips, 'shhh ...', give him a wink and close the door behind me, my conscience clear. After all, it was like that 'excuse for an affair' cheaters used – if his wife couldn't service his basic clothing and decorating needs, wasn't it okay for another female to step in and fill the gap?

Anyway, sorry, Mum B. I couldn't do it.

But at least I was daring enough to tell you the truth about why.

*

Mum B was right. Cheating in your head is complicated. Not to mention painful. I hadn't thought about that friend of my husband's for some time. We haven't seen her in at least six months. And now she will re-appear and I hate thinking about her. I hate it so much. She makes me feel like a fool without any options. She makes me feel like I'd put up with anything – that I am stupid and unseeing and trapped. I'm sure she didn't and doesn't think of me that way, but I can't help it. I probably will *never* be able to help it, because I'm not expecting that I will forget about her anytime soon. Not that it's about her; it's about my husband.

I don't blame Mum B for bringing up these feelings. All she's done is to pull back the edge of the tarp that hides the dark, locked-up storage facility in my mind where I keep the few things I prefer not to think about. But I'll be thinking about the affair that never was now – probably for some time. Which is, perhaps, a good thing. Sometimes you need a decent spring clean and that's what this anonymums caper is all about, really, isn't it? Unfortunately, there are times when spring cleaning is a little less feather dusting and more about hard core elbow-grease grime removal.

If that was my dare, I am more than slightly worried that my truth will be equally, if not more, depressing.

To: Mum A
From: Mum C
Subject: Truth

Dearest A,

We've finally met face-to-face. We've laughed. We've gotten a bit drunk. And teary. I know the smiling, friendly, engaging face that you present to the world.

Now I want to know the real you.

Take me inside your mind for a day. Tell me those secret thoughts you share with no-one else. Let me

January

> in on your inner monologue. Talk to me about what you're thinking when the kids smear peach on the lounge, despite you having given them a bowl, and a table and chair. Tell me what you'd really like to say to your mother-in-law when she tells you that she's given the kids three chocolate biscuits each before bed - just this once ... again.
>
> Crack the façade for me, Mum A. Vent a little.
>
> You know you want to.
>
> C

Oh boy, oh boy, oh boy. Why did no-one tell me about this before? It's not often you see a true breakthrough in motherhood. No, new and improved plasticware of any kind does not count, not even if it's Tupperware that the Tupperware lady tells you the astronauts use in space. But this ... this is a genuine breakthrough. Cheap, do it yourself, in your own time, at 3am if you want to, therapy. And what mum doesn't need that?

I've taken to venting with gusto, much like I'd eat the last brownie at playgroup after eyeing it off for half an hour. That is, I've hit the ground running and hoovered it up. It is just so, so good. So cathartic! All those things I've always wanted to say to my kids but kept bottled up inside, driving me nuts? Now I've found a way to purge myself. To get all those evil soul-destroying sentences out – out into a Word document, that is. I would never want to let them out for my family to hear, because my mother-in-law did that with her kids and the results weren't pretty (plus, by keeping things in, you save a lot of money on therapy, which can then be diverted to purchasing blue gin). But using Word is good. Once it's in Word, it's out of my head. I'm free! Plus, I can delete it, or perhaps keep it, saved in a secret location to present to my kids when they want to have a whinge about their *own* kids way down the track.

Within 24 hours of being 'truthed', I vented in several different documents in several different fonts and typefaces (one does like to be creative when it comes to bitching about one's offspring). And I haven't stopped at my kids. Oh, no. I've let it all hang out – there's no stopping me now. I could keep writing all night long! All week, even! But, for now, let us take a quick skip through just a few of the issues *du jour*:

The water bottle at playgroup

Listen, kid. I've just about had it with you pinching my water bottle. I'm cranky enough most of the time, so you don't want to see me cranky *and* dehydrated. I've taken the time to pack your own water bottle, the one that I went to great expense buying and even greater expense covering with those ridiculously priced personalised stickers. But do you want your own water bottle? No, of course you don't, you want mine. So, now that you've nicked off with it once more, of course you're going to do one of two things. Either you'll have a mouthful and pass it back (along with some lovely floaters), or you'll spill it. Oh, wait. There you go. Option B. Most of it's on the ground now and seeing as we're at playgroup, I'll have to give you the very boring 'don't waste water' speech like I have enough time to keep up with the daily percentage of water in our dams. I'll have to do it really loudly, too, so everyone can hear. Fantastic, you've also managed to spill three drops on your t-shirt in the process and we all know how you can't bear that, so we'll have to fish around in the baby bag with our fingers crossed in the hope that we've got another t-shirt for you to change into. Great, we don't. Stop screaming! It's three bloody drops of water! It's summer! It'll dry in less than a minute! Oh, all right, come here. Just to shut you up, I'll do the old mummy switcheroo [takes t-shirt off, puts back on back to front]. Honestly, haven't you cottoned on to this yet? Sometimes I wonder about you, child ...

The husband

I'm not going to say anything because that would be 'nagging'. No, instead, I'll just stand back and watch you in amazement, as we all get ready to go to the gym this fine Saturday morning. I use the term 'we' lightly, of course. Because 'we' in this case means that I get up at 6.30am, get the kids breakfast, give the cats some food, unload the dishwasher, load the dishwasher, put a load of washing on, hang a load of washing out, clean out the kitty litter, take out the rubbish and recycling, get the kids dressed, pack their snack for the gym crèche, write out the grocery shopping list for after the gym and get myself dressed. Then you get up at 8.10am, get yourself ready and make us both coffee. And then I have to thank you for the coffee, or I look like a bitch.

So, yeah, thanks for that delicious coffee, honey.

The eldest at the playground

Why do I bring you to the playground? You never want to play on any of the equipment! You're supposed to be running yourself ragged in the hope that I'll get an afternoon nap, but the only energy you ever expend is used frisking the baby bag for snacks. I can't believe that you have the audacity to get out of the car and run over to the playground, turn around, cross your arms and say, 'Wot you got?' Who taught you that choice phrase? Have you been watching *Eastenders* with Great-grandma? Stop searching through my bag like you're a customs inspector and get out of my wallet. Coins aren't for playing. Or for putting in your mouth. Or for choking on. See, I told you you'd choke. I told you you'd turn blue! No, you can't eat your brother's rusk. Don't take it from him. Here, eat this [passes banana to child]. I wouldn't want you to starve. After all, you've only had three bananas today and it's just gone 10am. When you explode, you're cleaning the mess up, understand? No, I told you not to run over to that dog. Wait for me [tries desperately to keep up, but is weighed down by stroller and baby bag]. Oh, what a lovely huge German shepherd. No, don't scream, it'll bite your head off. No, don't poke its anus, it'll *definitely* bite your head off. Oh, look, the dog's gone. But here's a baby. No, leave its dummy alone. You never wanted a dummy when you were a baby. Why do you want every dummy you see now that you're five? Oh, look, another over-sized dog. No, even though the 'nice lady' told you it's okay to pat her horse-sized hound, it does not mean it's okay to pat it. Just because it won't bite her arm off, doesn't mean it won't eat you in two mouthfuls. Especially when you poke it in the anus like that.

In the gym parking lot

What is it with door handles, kid? Why do you feel the need to test every single car door handle we go past? If I say, 'That's not your car' one more time, I think I'll have to be institutionalised. Oh, great. It must be the yummy mummies get tight tummies class at the gym today, because look at all the flash cars here this morning. Why are you drawn to testing out the handles on the most expensive cars with the loudest alarms? If this is your life's calling, why don't you go the whole hog, reach inside and pinch their mobiles while you're at it? Oh, yes, very funny. I like how you just pointed to the sleek convertible black Porsche, looked up at me and said, 'That's not your car, Mummy.' Hilarious. Like I'd be able to fit two kids, the groceries, the stroller and a vomiting cat that needs to be taken to the vet in that little number.

The mum from kindy

I know my daughter has a great love of food, a bit of a tummy and (ahem) quite a lot of gas, but after we've already seen a paediatric gastroenterologist, I'm thinking we don't really need your suggestion that 'maybe she has a food intolerance'.

Wow! Thanks! We never thought of that! We've only just been through the trial of excluding lactose and then through the fun of including it again and adding $5 sachets of probiotics to each serve of yoghurt she eats, but thanks for the heads up. Then again, maybe I shouldn't worry too much about what you think considering you just asked me if that Andy Warhol print on the wall is an original.

Toilet training

I've told you a million times before – you only get a Smartie when you do a poo in the toilet. Nothing else. A poo, understand? Not a wee, or a 'toot', as you so eloquently put it, but a poo. And no little goat-like nuggets like yesterday. I mean a proper poo. A Smartie-worthy poo. No, I don't think so. You know very well there's no poo under all that wasted toilet paper. There might be a whole lot of lack of sleep going on around here, but I'm not as dumb as I am tired, you know.

Mealtimes

No, you aren't getting a treat – you didn't eat any of your dinner. No, eating one bean does not count as eating dinner. This isn't Grandma's. No treat tonight. And don't ask your dad because he won't give you one either. Oh, wait, it looks like he will. How lovely for you. I should put both of you in the naughty corner, except 33 minutes in the naughty corner would be a treat for your father. He would probably take a good book, a packet of chips and have the time of his life.

Bedtime

[Three minutes after child is tucked up and chocolate is making an appearance from the depths of the pantry.] Hey! Stop that crying! You'll wake your brother up! What do you mean, 'Doggy'? Are you talking about that dog barking three streets away that I can barely hear? Anyway, it doesn't matter if there's a dog barking outside. It's 7.30pm and you're meant to be in bed, asleep. No, it doesn't matter if you can hear a possum, either. The possum can't get you. It's outside. So's the dog. They can't get in through the window. Yes, if it comes down to it, I'll save you. What? A crocodile? I can assure you there are no crocodiles out there. Yes, you're quite right. The dog and the possum and the crocodile, even though there definitely isn't one out there, should go to the naughty corner, together. Now what? You want what? Oh ... you want a kiss goodnight. Oh. All right, then, there you go. And a what? A pat? [Sigh.] Typical, you've broken me down again. It's very hard to be cross with you when you're sweet. Why can't you be naughty all the time? It would make life much easier when it comes to venting ...

*

My truth has been exciting me for days. Even after I'd sent it to the other two anonymums, I kept running back to the computer to vent like a thing possessed, writing things like 'you know, if you're going to write on the back of your brother's jumper and claim it wasn't you, it's best NOT TO WRITE YOUR OWN NAME', and so on. After day three of bolting to the computer with my verbal diarrhoea, I have to get myself to slow down, lest I become addicted to this wild behaviour. It was time to turn my attention elsewhere, so I'm turning it to Mum B. It's my turn to dare and I've been storing up a little something for her.

January

Mum B

My rut is changing shape. Not shallower, not deeper, but with an S-bend or two. For starters, I got away for a while. I ate mezze without having to give up the olives to Big Boy and feed Little Boy hummous off my pinkie finger. Part of me was very nervous about meeting up – it's hard to hide behind anonymity when everyone knows who you are, and boy, do they know more about my innermost thoughts than anyone has a right to know. But it gave me a lot to think about.

First, let's talk about sex. After talking to the others about the truth and its ramifications, I started thinking about that sexpert and her 'diarising'. Part of me recoiled – after all, if I schedule a bonk once a week after *Spicks and Specks*, aren't I just adding to the general ruttiness of my rut? But, frankly, it has to be better than the hit and miss approach that we've been using.

Unless you work at it, one of you is always going to be not 'in the mood'. Husband B gets up early and goes to bed early. I get up early and go to bed late. I really dislike morning sex. There, it's out there. Nothing will get me out of bed and dressed faster than an erection poking me in the back.

I'm sure I'm not alone in admitting that. Even if I am, I'm not reneging.

Husband B, on the other hand, like most men, is raring to go in the early hours, and asleep in front of the TV by 9.30pm. You could say we've been having a Circadian Rhythm Crisis.

So I decided I'd do a little scheduling. Like most working mums I tend to spend time on my computer at night, putting in 'extra time' to appease my guilt for leaving the office 'on time'. For three nights last week, my computer reminded me that it was 9.30pm. Each time, I walked away from the screen, seduced my husband silly, slipped out of bed once he was snoring, and went back to my tasks. It was actually fun in a slutty, service-your-needs kind of way.

I have no intention of keeping it up for three nights next week, but I'm going to try something different. For inspiration, I asked every mum I know – working or SAH – how she fits her relationship into her schedule. (Aren't you glad you're not one of my friends? I'm known for throwing these kinds of things out there.)

Mention sex to a group of mums and for the first few minutes all you hear is laughter. It's like telling a dirty joke, only there's no punch line and it's really not that funny. Then comes the response: what sex?

It occurred to me that many of our slang words for 'sex' and 'exhaustion' are actually interchangeable. Think about it: 'shagged', 'rooted', 'fucked' … All three can mean having sex or needing sleep. Anecdotal evidence suggests that the big joke (ah, now we get to it) for mums is that most are getting neither sex nor sleep!

Ha bloody ha.

I know that by the time you've worked through the 'must do' list of kids, work, homework, dinner, household chores, family commitments, household paperwork and all those other things that make up every day, you're hard-pressed to even find room on the sheet of paper for sex. All you want to do is to collapse into bed – and there's nothing worse than feeling like sex is just another thing that *has* to be done.

Pretty much everyone in the group started with that little diatribe.

But if you probe further, there's info to be found. The good thing about women is that they're completely indiscreet. I now know that several of my friends combine their sex life with their showering, killing two birds with one stone. Others have husbands with flexible jobs who can 'pop home' while the baby has a nap. One woman had taken the extreme step of not replacing the TV when it blew up – she said it leads to lovely quiet chats with a glass of wine and – hey presto!

Most said that even if they didn't feel like it, they could usually manage to 'get into it' once they got started. I'd like to point out that my friend Anais could be very useful in this situation!

What I notice when Husband B and I do get happy between the sheets is that the mood lifts in all other aspects of our lives. Generally, we get along well, laugh a lot and enjoy being with each other and our boys. In the aftermath of physical intimacy, though, it's all closer, friendlier, with a rosier glow.

Experts, including the aforementioned sexpert, would be waggling a finger at me right now, telling me not to confuse sex with intimacy. I don't. But I do know that sex can bring intimacy into a relationship when you both feel you are on parallel treadmills with a couple of rug rats running between you.

Anyway, it seems to be working for us.

So that's the first, and probably most obvious, S-bend.

The other is that I'm feeling more open. Down in a rut you can get very close-minded and old before your time. You start using phrases like 'breakdown of society' and 'youth of today'. You become more frightened of change. You worry about new things. You stop thinking about possibilities and start stressing about protecting what you've got.

When every day is the same, the slightest difference is blown out of proportion.

How did thinking about sexual fantasies help with this? Simple – it got me thinking about something out of the ordinary. No matter what you might think of me after reading my thoughts, the fact is that most days I don't go around fantasising about well-hung Russians or strangers on trains.

But I've been introduced to the frisson of excitement that thoughts can bring. So I've made another pact with myself. I'm going to make the time to read every day. Not a quick scan of the headlines online, or a gossip rag, or the endless catalogues that I find in the mailbox. Nope, I mean honest to God books.

And good ones at that, beginning with re-reading *A Room of One's Own*.

First, though, I'm going to check my In box. I'm hoping for a must-read email.

To: Mum B
From: Mum A
Subject: Dare

Mother B,

I am seeing Mum B as a girl who can take on the world without the help of brain and body rotting substances.

January

> This week, I'm making sure you'll be that girl. For one whole week, you will give up the two things that get us through the day - alcohol and 'treats.' (Don't pretend you don't know what 'treats' are - chocolate, lollies, chips, energy drinks etc. - all the things you hide from the other members of your family or at least wait till the kids are in bed to break out and share with your husband.)
>
> When you're done (if you survive, that is ...), let us know if it was easy, or hard. Do you feel better for it? Do you need these items as much as you think you do?
>
> Let us know so we don't have to do it!
>
> Mother A

If you'd asked me last week whether I had a drinking problem – or a Tim Tam problem, for that matter – I'd have laughed in your face. Me? Responsible mother of two, holder of job, keeper of grocery money, person in charge of everything? No way.

There are no vodka bottles stashed in my toilet cistern. No emergency sugar rations stuffed into the built-in wardrobe. Yes, there is the small matter of the cooking chocolate I tend to dip into when truly desperate, but really, I can stop any time I want.

Except now that I have to, I find I don't want to. Ever.

Every mum I know embraces 'wine time'. It popped up in all our lives about the same time as 'arsenic hour'. Seriously, how is anyone supposed to face 4–7pm with a small baby and no vino? I remember once flopping on to the couch, glass of wine in hand, in my pyjamas, at 7.05pm, with two small children asleep, and telling Husband B, seriously, that there was no better time of day.

Something about that glass of wine, or gin and tonic, or vodka and soda, or whatever your poison may be, restores your sense of yourself as an adult. It's not just the relaxing effect, that dulling of the senses that seems to take the shrillness out of a baby's cry. It's the idea of grown-up time being back in the house.

Treats are different. Treats are an all-day pick-me-up. A little something here and there to reward yourself for coping with the hell of it all – and for coping so *well*.

When you're breastfeeding, you can legitimately hoover up as many treats as you like. You're a factory, a machine, and you need fuel. Sticky, sweet, tasty fuel. And it doesn't seem to matter how much you suck in, because you know that baby will suck it out of you just as fast.

Except one day, it doesn't. And most of us don't notice. We continue taking in chocolate for 20, while the baby is only drinking enough milk for, well, one. People talk about the myth of breastfeeding being good for weight loss. It's not a myth, it's just not a never-ending story.

Unfortunately, habits are hard to break. I should know. I'm still fuelling my body for breastfeeding, despite the fact that I haven't lactated in nearly a year.

So I should embrace this challenge. I should look upon it

as a chance to reinvigorate my health and fitness. After all, research came out last year that said two standard drinks a day is damaging for women. Even the fact that they reviewed it this year and suggested that, actually, they were wrong and you could probably have four without drinking yourself into an early grave, didn't make me feel better. I don't know about you, but my wineglasses are fashionably bucket-like, so I'm probably getting through four standard drinks every time I pour myself a 'wee one'.

If nothing else, this might be an opportunity to lose weight. Make some inroads into the mummy tummy. God I hate that tummy. Adding the 'mummy' to it makes it sound cute. It's that whole 'yummy' thing all over again. But, you know what, it's a mum tum – and frankly that just sounds wobbly, don't you think?

Put like that, I'm more positive about this dare.

After all, it's not like it will be a problem.

Day 1

4pm
I'm so unbelievably good I should be beatified. Me and Mary MacKillop, Australia's first saints. I haven't so much as looked sideways at sweets all day and the wine thing is really not a problem. I never drink before 6pm and never on my own anyway. This is going to be a cinch.

6.30pm
Halos are overrated. Normally, I'd be pouring myself a nice cold glass of sauv blanc right now. Instead, I'm listening to my two little boys play 'Ben 10', which seems to involve a lot

of shouting, thumping, bumping, jumping and other tension-inducing noises. I'm realising that mothers of boys probably turn to self-sedation because it's illegal to administer soothing drugs to children. Boys buzz with energy. Even when they're not moving, there's a force field around them, bouncing off the walls, creating stress within anyone close by. That would be me.

But I'm okay, I don't really *need* a drink, I'd just like to have one.

8pm
They're finally gone and I'm on the couch contemplating an evening of non-ratings TV, with no promise of chocolate in the offing. I think I'll go to bed early.

Day 2

12 noon
Morning coffee with the girls is not the same without a friand. Particularly when the girls in question refuse to go out in sympathy and eat chocolate brownies in front of me, with relish. Little Boy is disconcerted when his regulation crumb or two doesn't materialise, and he puts on such a tantrum – roll on those terrible twos – that I buy him a friand to eat on his own. I contemplate licking up the crumbs, but it's not cool now, is it? I go home slightly cross.

7pm
The day has gone from bad to worse. Husband B fitted a new washing machine hose on the weekend. He swears he told me

January

that it needed to be tied to the tap or it will fall out of the sink and onto the floor ... but I swear he didn't. It doesn't matter. The fact is that the laundry disappeared under a tsunami of grey water at about 2pm and I couldn't even turn to a Tim Tam for consolation, nor a glass of wine for commiseration at the end of the day.

I hate this. I'm a normal person who likes an occasional glass of wine and a bit of chocolate. Why shouldn't I have them?

Because I take my dares seriously, that's why.

Day 3

8am
I have a headache. Could it be withdrawal? And, if so, from what?

More likely it's from hearing all about episode 24 of *Ben 10*. What happened to the Wiggles? That's what I'd like to know. Then, we knew where we were: a bit of Hot Potato, a rock or two of the bear, point your fingers, do the twist and jump in the Big Red Car. But now, I've got 'diamond-head guy' and 'four-arm guy' and eight other guys to deal with. If Big Boy actually knew anything about this cartoon, I wouldn't mind so much – but he's *never even seen the actual show*. I won't let him watch it because I think he's too young.

Instead, I am witnessing firsthand the power of word-of-mouth marketing. Kids, it turns out, are naturals at it. Some kid came to pre-school with an enormous plastic omnitrix-watch-thingy, and voila! The Game Has Changed.

I contemplate this notion over a very strong cup of coffee. Thank God the fun police didn't remove caffeine as well. Do I want the Tim Tam because I'm conditioned by marketing to want the Tim Tam? Or do I want the Tim Tam because it's so chocolatey and crunchy, and so perfect with a cup of coffee?

I plump for the latter. I am too grown up to succumb to advertising. Perhaps I can ring up that dishy guy from *Gruen Transfer* – now there's a thinking woman's crumpet – and ask him. Todd Something. I'll go and look him up. It might stop me thinking about Tim Tams.

3pm
I am sitting writing this because if my fingers are typing they cannot be creeping towards the cupboard. In desperation I am considering finishing off the boys' stash of Jelly Dinosaurs. Only the thought of the disappointment (and screaming) that would ensue should there not be one waiting for Big Boy's arrival home from pre-school is stopping me. But I'm not sure how long I'll consider that a deterrent.

8pm
Hi, my name is Mum B, and I have a drinking problem. My problem is that I can't have one. And I want one ... I do.

Day 4

9am
Husband B has started up again with his seachange/treechange/mechange thing. He's been going on about it for some time now, on and off. He'll bring it up, then not talk about it again for a month. Right when I think he's forgotten

about it all, he'll try me again, just to keep his foot in the door. And now, he's chosen the one day that I have at home by myself to ambush me with a phone call. I do not want to think about starting my life again somewhere else. I particularly do not want to deal with the anxiety it brings whilst I'm without my twin crutches of sugar and alcohol.

I have come to realise just how much I rely on them. Not in any huge fashion, but in a very constant fashion.

This dare is turning out to be way more confronting than I had imagined.

And I'm not losing any weight!

6.30pm
We have just returned from a family walk. I decided that half the trouble with the witching hour is the routine of it. We do the same things because we do the same things, if you know what I mean. So I reach for the wine simply because I'm there, it's there and everyone else is there, usually whingeing or screaming.

Tonight I put them both in the pram with a little lunch box full of picnic-style delights and told them that dinner would be a moveable feast. They were delighted.

Husband B and I had a serious but casual conversation *en route* about this whole move business. I cautiously told him, at the end of an hour's walking with endorphins flooding my bloodstream, that I would consider it.

I like the walking thing. I think we'll do more of that. There's an intimacy in it. Intimacy without pressure because nobody's going to leap on you for sex while you're walking around the block with two kids. Having said that, I could go a bonk right now. I'm in a happy place.

Day 5

10pm
Friday night is hard for a sober person. Husband B came in, cracked a beer, put his feet up and prepared for the usual *Better Homes & Gardens* takeaway/wine combination that marks out the Friday nights of most mums and dads around the country. (Don't get me started on Saturday night and *The Bill* – we're lost without it.) Somehow it lost all its appeal without the haze of a good cab sauv to give it a rosy glow.

I went to bed early only to avoid the temptation of the box of chocolates my beloved brought home with him to celebrate our 'breakthrough conversation' last night.

Day 6

See Day 5. Only now there's less than half a box of choccies left as Husband B set out on a mission to save me from myself.

Day 7

Well, I've done it. I've lasted a week and it's been a real eye-opener for me. I didn't know how hard it would be. I didn't know how dependent I'd become. Most of the women I've talked to this week about my challenge shuddered at the very thought of it, so I know I'm not alone.

The good news is that I've lost weight. The bad news is that I'll probably put the 400g back on as soon as I pour my first glass of wine. But that won't be until Thursday. I've

January

set myself a new rule – no alcohol from Sunday to Thursday. Treats are back on the menu, but not every day and not when I think it's a habit thing (3pm anyone?). I've decided to buy those little individual packs of Crunchies and Cherry Ripes and limit myself to one or two after dinner each night. No more open packets of Tim Tams in the fridge – it's too damn easy to slip one from the pack every time you open the door.

It's not exactly sainthood. But I reckon I'll feel better for it.

I'm wondering how many women would be shocked at how they would feel if they'd been asked to complete that dare. Alcohol makes the news in our country regularly for a reason. On the whole, we drink too much. Even mums who think they don't drink much at all.

I admit that I got a shock when I went to the doctor's last week. A new doctor, so we had to go through all that history stuff. When I told him, feeling incredibly virtuous, that I only drink a few nights a week now, he nodded. Then he asked me what my history was like. I had to admit that in my 20s I could drink a rugby team under the table. He wrote 'former binge drinker' on my history. Sobering. Makes me sound like Amy Winehouse, if somewhat more reformed.

Anyway, I'm never going to be a teetotaller, but I'm also never going to drink without awareness like I have been doing. As for the chocolate/treat situation, I guess it's the same. It's been mindless, and now I'm aiming for mindfulness.

Speaking of mindful, I'm mindful of the fact that my truth is due any minute. Given the number of truths my dare brought home to roost, I feel I should be let off on this – like a two for one thing – but I know my partners in crime will not be so generous.

In fact, that could be the siren song of incoming mail that I hear right now ...

> **To: Mum B**
> **From: Mum C**
> **Subject: Truth**
>
> Dear little detoxed one,
>
> Mum A has told us the truth about one mother. Now it's your turn to squirm in the parenting hot seat. What do you do (or not do, or simply believe, as the case may be) that, if it were known by the masses, would bring down the wrath of the Mums' Group on you? You must have at least one unpopular view you can tell us about. Come on, spill. We won't judge you. Much.
>
> Yours in feigned superiority,
>
> Mum C

These tasks aren't getting any easier. There's nothing like taking away a girl's sauv blanc and making her a traitor to her sex to take her out of her comfort zone. Give me a five-things-about-men-that-drive-me-nuts task and I could riff for hours – without even getting into the old toilet-seat-up cliché. We all could. It's so much easier to point the finger at the other team. But when it's your own side ... well, now, that makes it a whole different ball game.

It's not that I think women are perfect, far from it. We've all suffered the slings and arrows of random bitchiness, gossip and plain *Mean Girls*-style torture. But I'm not perfect either, so who am I to spill the beans on the sisterhood?

January

But a truth is a truth, so I've reluctantly come up with not one view, but a list. It's not easy even writing this list. But putting them down on paper has one benefit – it's like therapy, without the hefty price tag.

1. Every one of us says how much we despise judgmental women - right before we pass judgment on another woman

There exists, somewhere in the family photo collection, an ugly, ugly photo of my sister and me, caught unawares at a formal function. It's not that we look like sisters of the Elephant Man – on the contrary, we are ten years younger, slim, and looking as good as 90s fashion allows. Nope, the ugliness is in the expression on our faces – we are both looking into the distance with a 'fuck, would you look at that!' expression. Whether we'd caught sight of a random pop-up G-string, a mutton-dressed-as-lamb exhibit, a take-me-home-and-fuck-me-actually-just-fuck-me-now slut-fest, or, possibly, The Wrong Shoes outrage, it doesn't matter. You can't see it. All you can see is the judgment written all over our faces.

There are two reasons why I won't throw it out. First is I should hold on to it to remind myself just how unattractive judgment is. Second is the family photos are so disorganised that it's unlikely I'll find it because it's probably been filed with my younger brother's baby photos.

Women do not understand the meaning of live and let live. Instead we follow the theory that you can live, but you have to live the way I think you should. Take the whole stay-at-home mums (SAHM) versus working mums debate. We waste countless inches of magazine column space, countless hours of media air time and countless days of our lives talking about which is the best option. Each side has its own manifesto about why their way is the only way to produce happy kids.

Instead of coming together to ensure that *all* women can choose to raise their kids the way they want to, we splinter our efforts, ensuring that no-one is completely satisfied. God forbid that you should turn up at the school gate in tracksuit pants and a t-shirt (not counting designer velveteen numbers). You wouldn't get past the cargo-pants and ironed-shirts (or whatever the uniform is at your school) wall of judgment to be able to find your kid. If you haven't lost your baby weight three minutes after the birth, some 'kind' woman will be handing over her diet tips and a Pilates DVD.

Helpful? Possibly. More helpful would be a cup of tea and a chat about how you're going. My sister and I made different decisions about how we were going to raise our kids. Do I judge her when I see her children acting out for attention? Hell, yes! Does she judge me when she sees that I'm neglecting myself and my relationship in the chaos of my family? Absolutely. Does it help either of us? Not a bit. I think it's time to find that photo. If for no other reason than it was probably the last time we were in complete agreement.

2. We don't appreciate what we have

Once upon a time, I was a tall, slim girl with fantastic tits, fair skin and long bouncy hair. When I was that girl, I didn't appreciate any of it. I hated the fact that I was a size 12, not a 10. I hated the fact that guys talked to my breasts instead of my face. I hated the fact that I was the whitest person in the room – any room.

And I hated the fact that my hair frizzed at the slightest hint of humidity – pretty much every day of the year.

Nowadays, I look at pictures of that girl and all I can think is 'what a waste'. Why didn't I wear bikinis and mini skirts and boob tubes every single day of my life? Why didn't I get my belly button pierced and my breast tattooed, and flaunt both of them (well, maybe not the breast so much, and probably not both the belly button and breast at the same time). Now that my hair is showing signs of grey, my tits are somewhere around my unpierced belly button, and my slimness is taking a while to resurrect itself from the last pregnancy, all that's left of that girl is the 'tall' and the 'fair skin'.

My point? We spend so much time angsting about what we don't have that we forget to appreciate what we do.

Romance is another area where we tend to miss the point. I have a friend who whinges every year that her man fails to send her roses on Valentine's Day. This is the same guy who buys her flowers every couple of weeks 'just because', who gets her car serviced, who gave her a small key for her key ring to remind her that she had the 'key to his heart' – this is one romantic guy! But not according to her. And all because she has to watch her work colleagues receive overpriced roses on one day of the year while she receives none.

3. We allow ourselves to be defined by shoes

Confession time: shoes are not my life.

I'm a 39-year-old woman who has worked in the city her whole adult life. I have lived in London, been to New York and

Paris, even had a brief flirtation with the exotic in Istanbul. In fact, if my life were a book, it would probably be a chick-lit novel (right up until the bit where she lived happily ever after, then, thanks to kids, it turns into a horror story).

All that, and not one pair of Manolo Blahniks or Jimmy Choos. I know, so not *Sex and the City*. So ... not.

I've tried, I really have. I go shopping. I visit 17 shoe shops in a single lunchtime, examining every pair closely. Everything I see fits in the category of 'too high', 'too bronze', 'too Gold Coast', 'too wedgey'. Or 'not wedgey enough', 'not strappy enough', 'not the slightest bit comfortable'.

As a consequence, I have a paltry seven pairs of shoes. One pair of trainers, one pair of the world's-most-comfortable sandals, one pair of high-but-not-ridiculous sparkly strappy sandals, one pair of Gisele-Bundchen-esque leather thongs, one pair of slides, one pair of wedges, one pair of flat black boots. (You'll note the Netherlands landscape – no Everest heels here.)

Sad but true.

Not for me those little shoe storage boxes with Polaroids on the outside for easy identification – my little collection fits neatly under my bed, side by side.

Given that this is one area in a woman's life where size really matters, the paltry nature of my shoe wardrobe should cause me angst. You can't open a women's magazine without having the shoes-are-good message rammed home. One fashion mag. even offers readers the choice – the shoes or the outfit. Spend $2000 on a pair of Gucci platform heels, or, for the same amount, get a whole ensemble – including two pairs of shoes! Oh, the dilemma – not.

But I'm not the only woman in the world who doesn't get

all breathless at the sight of a pair of heels. So why do we all pretend? Why have we allowed ourselves to be the sum of our shoes? Why don't we tell those fashion mag. hags, who think it's perfectly okay to wear a skirt as a top and a belt as a hat, that we have had enough. Shoes are just one part of the outfit, and just one small part of our lives. Even if they are the only thing that fits every time we try them on.

4. We are competitive

To me, there's only one reason that women aren't running the planet. It's the same reason that it's rare for a woman to be the sole survivor on the *Survivor* TV show. We're too competitive. We talk a good game, banging on about sisterhood and being there for each other, but the truth is, even when we have the numbers, the backstabbing and bitching between us allows a man to cut through the middle and go straight to the winner's podium.

I thought it was bad enough when I was young and single. Older women in the office who should have been mentors were too busy wondering if my young face made their wrinkles stand out more to help me make sense of the male-dominated workplace. I understand it now (though I didn't then), but I still don't like it.

Now that I'm a mum, however, the competition has become world-class. If I've learned anything, it's never to get between a woman and her belief that her kid is Gifted and Talented (G&T). I had no idea that parenting was a blood sport until Big Boy showed a talent for talking. I was proud of his prowess, but kind of wished he'd shut up occasionally, especially at the playground. One time at the playground a woman with a mad glint in her eyes bailed me up to find out what I was 'doing with him at home to help his talking'. Er, nothing except talking to him, really – no flash cards, no Baby Einstein, no tutor.

You could tell she didn't believe me. But she took it on the chin and started bragging about how her kid walked at three months, grew teeth at six days, and rolled over on his way out of the uterus. I'd look at my sweet little 15-month-old boy, who could ask you what time it was (like he had an appointment), but who was still crawling, and who didn't sit up until about nine months because he seemed to know that if he lay on his lardy arse people would bring the toys to him. And I'd ask him to start counting the rungs on the slippery slide ladder.

What was it I was saying about being competitive?

5. We don't talk straight

I consider myself to be a pretty straight-talking gal. If you asked me if your bum looked big in your jeans, I'd tell you. If your skirt was so short we were practically sharing a Britney moment, I'd comment. But if you piss me off really badly, chances are I'd not tell you – I'd tell everyone else we know.

It's a confrontation thing. Husband B is constantly accusing me of saying one thing when I mean another. When I say, 'Oh well, best I wash up for the 15th time today, so why don't you lie on the couch and relax?' and then stomp around, crashing pans, he follows me to the kitchen and says, 'I sense that you would prefer that I do this. Why didn't you just say so?' Actually he says, 'Why are you making so much damn

January

noise?' and I let rip at him about how he never washes up and I do everything and the kids are driving me crazy and the washing machine's broken down again and ... well, you get the picture. At which point he says, 'Why didn't you just say so? I can't read your bloody mind.' Which is a fair point.

Women are great talkers. We're just not very good at saying what we really think, which is why I think that every single one of us should undertake this exercise.

It's a great way of finding out some truths about yourself.

*

Oh My God, I hope no-one ever cracks Mum B's true identity. I'd be toast.

Mum C spoke of 'at least one unpopular view' and somehow, in no time, five spilled forth. I want to take it all back. I do. But I'm not going to because it's the truth. Well, as I see it anyway. This game has taken me into some dark, soul-searching places. This truth took me there too. One place I didn't imagine I'd end up was thinking about miscarriage – but I did. I rarely voice my views about this difficult area of motherhood because I know that I'm not in step with current thinking. In the end, I didn't include it in my final five, because I realised, thinking it through, that it's an area where there simply is no one-size-fits-all answer. In fact, most areas of motherhood fall into the same category.

There was a huge kerfuffle in the mothering community last year when a perfectly coiffed journalist had the hide to suggest that motherhood was a lark and that we should all get over ourselves. I admit I threw that particular article across the room when I first read it. Who the hell was she to say such a thing?

Then I thought a bit more about it and I realised I agreed a little bit. As I've said before, it's hard to talk about the good stuff in motherhood. You get sweet and sentimental. Much funnier and self-deprecating is to discuss what crap it all is. Few mums shy away from an opportunity to share horror stories; start discussing how cool your kid is, however, and they'll look at you like you're boasting.

This train of thought took me through some interesting landscapes, including thinking about miscarriage. Why? Because I'd once felt ostracised because of my views on a subject pertaining to motherhood, just like that journalist.

I read somewhere that one in four pregnancies end in miscarriage. Often this will happen before the mother even knows she's pregnant, resulting in a heavy period. But this is not always the case.

I had my first miscarriage when Big Boy was a little over 12 months old. I was 10 weeks pregnant – only I wasn't. I woke one morning to spotting, was at the doctor by 8.30am and an ultrasound at 10am revealed – nothing. There was no baby. Medically, this is known as 'blighted ovum'. The pregnancy ends so early that the body doesn't even have time to register that it's all over. So it continues to produce pregnancy hormones and all the symptoms of pregnancy. Sore boobs, morning sickness, extreme fatigue. I had all that. Just no baby.

Lying on the ultrasound table, looking at the empty space where my baby should have been, was the strangest feeling of my entire life. I was unsure of what to do next. Did I cry? Did I scream? I did neither of these things. Either would have felt like shutting the gate after the horse had bolted. The baby had been gone for weeks. I would have been grieving for just an empty space.

January

I got up, went out to the waiting room where Husband B was waiting with Big Boy, and calmly informed him that we weren't having a baby. On the way home, I explained to him what had happened. We both agreed that we were shocked and numb – but unsure of what to do next.

Three hours later, I went to an Ob/Gyn, who booked me in for a 'procedure to remove the products of pregnancy'. A D&C. I could have waited for those products to remove themselves of their own accord, but she explained that this might take weeks. Weeks of walking around with that empty space inside me.

Two days later, it was done. My pregnancy was officially over. And I was okay. Really okay. Something had gone wrong with that baby, really wrong. I explained this over and over to family members and the few friends I'd told. We hadn't announced the pregnancy at that stage – we are very much old school like that, waiting for 12 weeks. I was glad about that. It wasn't so much that I would have had difficulty with having to tell more people what had happened, just that everyone who did have to be told seemed to have so much difficulty with me. I spent a lot of time reassuring other people, trying to make *them* feel better about my loss. It was exhausting.

At the time, I didn't know too many women who'd experienced a miscarriage. Nobody in my circle had been there. (Part of me thought, well, I'm the one in four, so hopefully none of my close friends will go through this.) I wasn't sure how I was supposed to feel. I felt terribly sad, of course, but also some relief. If there was something wrong with the baby, I was happy that nature had taken its course rather than subject us both to a lifetime of pain and suffering. I also had Big Boy to think about, which meant that I didn't have much time for thinking anyway. I got on with things. Like so many women had done before me.

People kept telling me how well I was doing, in a surprised tone of voice. Sometimes that tone bordered on accusatory (not, I hasten to add, from close friends and family). One friend told me about a friend of hers who'd miscarried at six weeks and gone to bed for three weeks, unable to get past the sadness. I began to wonder if I should be doing things differently. Was I not sad enough? Should I have been in a worse state? Was I cold and unfeeling and not caring enough?

Curious, I went online to see what others thought, Googling miscarriage. I found forum after forum dedicated to the subject. I went in, turned around and got the hell out as quickly as possible. I knew instantly that I didn't fit in. The forums were full of women talking about their Angel Babies (the ones who did not make it).

As I read, I empathised with them in their grief. It is horrible to lose a baby at any stage. The loss is not just of the pregnancy, but of the excited expectation of the life that you were going to share with the child. But even as I read, I knew that, while we'd shared a similar experience, I couldn't do what they were doing. It was what everyone seemed to want to see from me, but changing the way I was dealing with my loss for everyone else's benefit was pointless.

While I lost two babies (the second at 15 weeks), I cannot tell you the date of either of those losses. I choose not to remember because that is my way. Every year, around the months that they occurred, I am unaccountably sad, like my body remembers even if my mind does not. The Mothers' Love rose that I planted blooms its pretty pink flowers every summer, a beautiful tribute to the babies that never were. I smile when I see them.

One of them was a little girl. My only chance for a little girl. I would have loved a little girl. But it was not to be. She did not survive. It happens. But I have two boys, beautiful, healthy, lively little boys. I am blessed. I want to focus my attention on that, rather than feeling defined by the saddest thing that ever happened to me.

After my first miscarriage, I asked my doctor how long I would need to wait until I tried again. Six weeks. The body recovers and gets ready to start again. Within three months, I was pregnant. Not successfully. Three months later, I was pregnant again.

Four pregnancies. Two children. I won't get pregnant again. At 39, I think I'm too old, and losing two babies is enough for anyone. Just because I don't light candles for them, or write them up in my email signature doesn't mean I don't see them every day in the gap between my two boys.

For me, there is such a thing as talking too much about the bad stuff. So I don't talk about it. This is my choice. I will listen to you talk about your experiences, empathise with you, cry with you if you need me to do so. But I won't share mine. I will tell you that I lost two babies and then I will change the subject. When I do this, don't assume for one second that it's because I'm heartless and don't care. I do. I care as much as you do. It's just that I'm doing it in my own way.

You see why this is not on my list. Everyone's reaction to the bad stuff is personal and, taking my own advice from point one, I'm not judging anyone. All I ask is the same in return.

*

I must say, I like this straight talking. I don't do enough of it. I tend to run from confrontation, but finally, after nearly 40 years on the planet, I feel ready to stand up for myself. Maybe it's having kids. You need to stand up for them, and if you can't stand up for yourself first ...

Speaking of which, it's time to come up with a stand-up, straight-talking truth challenge for Mum C. One that will make her squirm as much as I just have. It will need to be big, bigger than Ben Hur, bigger than ... oh wait, I know just the thing. What's bigger than the planet?

Poor Mum C.

January

Mum C

Busy busy busy! Things have been hectic around here. I have assignments due, the little one has hospital appointments, the big one is stressing out about downsizing at work and my in-laws are nuts.

No, really, they are.

I barely survived Christmas with them. They didn't celebrate Christmas on the 25th, when it's, you know, Christmas day. They decided instead to have it on the 27th because they are nuts. If you have a better explanation, feel free to enlighten me. Until then, I am sticking with the nuts theory. It's a good theory and it works for all sorts of situations. Observe:

> 'Why won't she just put on a pair of socks if her feet are cold?'
> 'Because she's nuts.'
> 'Why is she buying all those clothes that will never fit her?'
> 'Because she's nuts.'
> 'Why is he putting his bowl of porridge on his head?'
> 'Because he's nuts.'

It also saves me time on coming up with Dr Phil-esque analyses.

There is something that's been driving *me* nuts – I've noticed a distinct trend lately. There are an awful lot of pregnant women around. It seems that everywhere I turn, there is either a squeaky little newborn or a nicely ripened pregnant woman. Much as I know other women hate it (I wasn't fussed either way, really), it's all I can do to stop myself from running over and rubbing their bellies, asking them when they are due and being surprised by whatever date they tell me (it's always too late or too early!), asking them if they know what they are having and whether they have picked out names yet.

It's all terribly intrusive but I can't help myself. I suppose I'm nuts.

It's a strange headspace I'm in, actually. I want to have access to a baby but I don't want to be pregnant. Oh, no. I remember the pain and stress all too well. After all that lumbering around, feeling like a lead-filled beach ball, having to go to the toilet every 2½ seconds and having hormones charging through your body, making you cry because someone said all the strawberry milk has gone, and then you have to deal with birthing the babe.

But, as my boy gets older, there's a shift in my body and I am finding my heart arguing with my head. I want a baby, says the heart. Bugger off, says the head.

How to decide that one? And let's not forget there's another party involved – it's about 'we,' not just 'me'.

I think what really irritates me most about my husband as a co-parent is his use of the word 'we'. It began when 'we', apparently, were pregnant. Funnily enough, I never saw him hurtling to the loo to chuck his guts up every 30 seconds. Nor did I see him suffer the lower back pains as the baby grew.

When 'we' were in labour, I don't recall him feeling like a hundred scarabs were trying to eat their way out from his abdomen. Nor do I remember anyone asking him to drop his pants and having a good peer up his jacksy.

With the birth finally over, 'we' were now breastfeeding, but the he in 'we' was definitely absent from the breasts-so-tender-that-sneezing-makes-you-cry club. So where were his tortured nipples and sleepless nights?

'We' were getting up to him four times a night, (No, no, dear, you were *woken* four times a night. Turning over and emitting a muffled hhmmfffpph? noise before falling back to sleep does not in any way, dear, constitute 'getting up to him'.)

'We' were doing great. Of course 'we' were! Ignore the fact that the house looked like a bomb had hit it, that I was wearing underwear that was falling off me because I was still wearing maternity knickers and couldn't get out to buy new underwear, that my plants were all dead and that the faint smell of yoghurty desperation had become my existence. Oh yes, 'we' were doing just great!

Our latest 'we' is that 'we' are toilet training. While on my hands and knees, scrubbing toddler wee from the carpet, I heard him say to his mother on the phone that 'we' take him to the toilet periodically through the day but 'we're' not rushing things. There are accidents, sure, but 'we' are dealing with them. He was genuinely surprised when a urine-soaked sponge came hurtling his way from across the room.

Later on that week he told me he had been thinking that maybe we should have another baby. The little one isn't so little anymore. 'We' could cope.

Two hours of hysterical screaming later, he nodded sagely, said he understood my concerns and that 'we' would find a way to work everything out. Sometimes he makes it really bloody hard to be a pacifist.

After all that we-ing and weeing, I was ready for some surreptitious me-ing. I checked my email every day for a week only to discover an empty Inbox. Then one day, I had mail.

To: Mum C
From: Mum A
Subject: Dare

Dear Sister in Motherhood,

I've heard a rumour that you and your husband are not of a particular religious persuasion. But motherhood is tough. We could all use a little help. Maybe even of the divine kind. So, get ready to turn your eyes to the wonder of the Lord for inspiration and salvation.

Fire up the pay TV, for you will be locking your dial on the Christian Television station and you will be transfixed. Every spare moment you have, you will sit on your couch and take in the joys of Hillsong et al. You will let your husband see your new-found interest. Feel free to invite friends over for Tea'n'Hymn sessions. Learn what it feels like to be one of the newly saved. Fend off the cynics who question your fledgling faith. Convince those

> closest to you that you will soon be affixing a fish sticker to your car.
>
> And then tell all.
>
> Yours,
>
> The ever-saintly A

Goodness me, how did they know? Had I mentioned something? Did they shape this dare just for my husband or was it pure bad luck on my part? The email stared back at me, mocked me, dared me.

My husband is an atheist. He once was an apathetic soul, who didn't much care what people believed, thought people who believed in God were all rather quaint and comical, like people who scrapbook or knit little toilet roll covers in atrocious multicoloured wool to keep themselves entertained and, hopefully, off the streets. Good for them. Of course, he no more believed in the object of their worship than he did in the pot of gold at the end of a rainbow, but if they wanted to look heavenwards and ask for Old Mother Gregory's sponge cake to fail spectacularly just ahead of the church fete, well that was between them and their ceiling fan.

That all changed a few years ago. I'm not quite sure what happened, but he went from an agreeable atheist to a full tilt, fire-breathing heathen. You couldn't relate a cute little tale about a child saying 'Godidit' when caught out in conducting some mischief without heavy eye rolling and a rant about the indoctrination of children. If you slipped up and said 'bless you' when someone sneezed, more ranting and raving. And heaven forbid he should see any example of religion encroaching on the business of the state. It doesn't matter how much I agree with him, when he's in the ranting zone, he's in the ranting zone. It's easier for me to make a cup of tea, grab a piece of cheesecake and resign myself to his rants.

So, dear bored fellow mums, you know not what you ask with this dare. Rather than alleviating my mundane daily grind, you are daring me to add to it, significantly. And all for your own amusement, no less.

A dare is a dare. And the bored must accept. So here I am, beginning my misery in three parts.

The first act of the dare held quite a surprise. I waited until the child was sleeping and settled down to an evening on the couch, finally able to change the channel away from the antics of Dora. I flicked past the endless reruns of *Law and Order*, past awful home makeovers, past Martha Stewart (vaguely wondering if she decanted prison dishwashing liquid into attractive glass containers, too) and locked on to the Christian Channel. Watching my husband out of the corner of my eye, I suppressed the grin that was dying to break out while keeping myself firm in my resolve to sit through the onslaught that was about to begin any moment now. He walked through the lounge room to a chorus of 'Hallelujah!' and I tensed all over. His eyes flicked from the TV to my intent face and back to the TV.

'What are you watching?'

Oh dear, full words. No contractions. This sounds bad.

'Oh, just this new Christian channel.'

'Why?'

January

I shrugged. I didn't have a prepared answer because I hadn't expected a question. A rant, certainly, but not a question.

He looked on for a few moments and walked away without a word. As if that wasn't shock enough, he walked into the kitchen and started on the dishes! Goodness, all these years of nagging, begging and pleading and all I had to do was turn over to some awful evangelising? Halle-fricken-lujah, indeed!

Day two. Buoyed by the overwhelming success of the previous night (granted, not a success for my darers but come on, he did the dishes *and* wiped down the counters! I'm on the brink of a spiritual awakening, here!), I sat back with a mug of hot chocolate and opted for a program about living life with peace and joy, basking in the glory and light of God. My husband trundled in, looked at the TV and asked, 'What are you watching that crap for?' I shushed him, feigning complete engrossment in the program, sitting forward, peering at the screen, taking slow and deliberate sips of my drink. I'd actually practised this during the day, the leaning forward, the peering, the slow and quiet movements, the eyes barely wavering from the screen. I even had some nodding and murmuring planned but omitted these during dress rehearsal just before he came home. Honestly, pathetic as it may sound, all that practice gave me quite a thrill. Here I was, the Cate Blanchett of the mummy world, about to take my Oscar-deserving plunge! The final performance went off flawlessly. I must have been convincing as he tutted quietly and deposited himself on the couch next to me to glare at the TV.

I had obviously glazed over a bit, lost in my own thoughts of what toilet paper to buy tomorrow and how I could possibly justify buying another box of chocolate chip cookies, so, when it happened, the noise to my right made me start. It took me a moment to realise that he wasn't hurling abuse at the TV as I had initially thought but was actually laughing. Not knowing what he was laughing at, I started to watch the program properly. Perhaps it was amusing; there's no reason it wouldn't be, considering it was about love and peace and joy and all. But no, he wasn't laughing, he was hooting. I fell into my role and shushed him, again feigning a pressing interest in the words of the kindly man on the screen (though, in truth, I was more interested in what possessed him to wear such a jumper) but my infantile husband was not to be deterred. He laughed at the perfectly proper words that the man used by taking them out of context, like 'cock', for example – 'I tell you the truth,' Jesus said, 'this very night, before the *cock* crows, you will disown me three times.' He laughed at the affirmations while quoting some of his own, like 'Throw your daughters out to be raped by the angry mob that comes seeking your guest – you will be blessed mightily for it!' On and on he went and, I'm afraid, I crumbled. There was only so much my poor sleep-deprived head could take and soon we were both sitting on the couch laughing at the poor man and his awful clothing.

*

I decided to give my husband a few days' peace, lest he have an aneurism, or take steps towards institutionalising me. It was a couple of days after the puddles of laughter incident when I thought it was time to try again. This time, I clicked straight to the channel, no pausing, no perusing. I was businesslike – brusque and no nonsense. Yes, I had practised that too. And yes, it had given me a slight thrill.

The program was about humanitarian efforts made by some church or other, where the parishioners donated money, food, blankets and time to the local soup kitchen. The plight of the homeless people was heart breaking. Families on the street because they had fallen through the welfare gaps. Families living under bridges. Parents scraping together everything they could in order to keep their loved ones together. My husband watched the program with me without comment, without laughter or hooting. It was a sobering program, bringing to light just how astonishingly lucky we were to have our son tucked up warm and safe in his cot, to have a roof over our heads and cupboards full of food.

For all the distrust and dislike I have for The Church as an institution, if it encouraged people to help the unfortunate, surely that was at least one point in its favour? I put this view to my husband. 'Not really,' he retorted, telling me they were only helping others out of selfishness. And so began the discussion I had been awaiting for nearly a week. Far from being a dragging bore, it was actually a relief – not just because it had finally arrived but also because we both touched on the things we had just seen, revitalising the same old argument (the one we've had for years), giving it new life. We eventually took our argument to the bathroom, snapping at each other between toothpaste spits.

'What does it matter why they're doing it?' I said, after a good spit. 'At least there are more blankets on the street for the cold homeless.'

'That's all very well but they don't really give a stuff about the homeless,' he said, spitting as well. 'It's all about making themselves feel better.'

'So they feel better,' I shrugged between flosses. 'They feel all moral and upright, and the homeless feel warmer. What's the big deal?'

'Because intent matters,' he replied, charmingly blowing his nose and then inspecting the tissue. 'Because they aren't doing it to be good people, they're doing it because they think it will get them into heaven. It's mercenary.'

'But intent matters only to people who are warm in their homes! I wouldn't give a stuff about why someone was handing me a blanket if I was freezing, any more than I would wonder why someone was throwing me a life ring when I was drowning.'

Tucked in under the covers and still bickering a bit, he asked me why I was watching that show in the first place and what was with all those Christian programs lately. Oh, how glad I was that he asked me that in the pitchy dark!

'Just sort of getting into the whole thing. It's really interesting. Makes sense.'

'Yeah, right.'

'No really! Don't you think it makes sense? There's something to it all that just speaks to me.'

I could feel the glare even though I couldn't see it.

Since then, I've been singing hymns around the house. It always makes him pause briefly. I wonder if he's thinking if I could do a complete 180 degree turn and suddenly take up a crucifix. Though the confusion could be to do with my song choices – barring the first dozen or so words of 'Amazing Grace', the only hymns I know the words to are Christmas carols.

It's a wonderful, comforting feeling to really know the person you love, to know what they believe and who they are. I know my husband. I know what he believes, I know his buttons, his hot topics, what makes him laugh. I also know he knows me. We've been together for many years and share a child; there's nothing about either of us that surprises the

January

other anymore. Gone are the days of, 'Oh, really? I didn't know that!' But I've now discovered that a lot of satisfying fun and hedonistic delight can be had from messing with his head. And knowing him as well as I do, there is no-one else in the world that can mess with him to the same degree. What fun!

Perhaps I'll hang a set of rosary beads on the bed rail, and see where we go from there.

*

It's funny how leading your husband off kilter can make things fresh and new. We hadn't been talking for a while. We spoke, sure, asked each other to pass the bread, shared a funny story or related a news piece to the other, but generally he would be at his computer, reading his nerdy articles, while I was at mine, buggering around on Facebook while pretending to be working. Since the dare, he's been asking me things, not just telling me about something. He's been seeking out my opinion more, like he used to when we first met. Though he has no doubt worked out that my spiritual awakening deserves at most a cynical eye roll, he still asks what I think about this or that issue.

And guess what? Asking about one thing leads to asking about another. We'd fallen out of the habit of asking, because we were so sure we knew each other completely and didn't realise that the asking wasn't just about the knowing, it was also about showing interest, care and that the other person matters.

I was serious about picking up some rosary beads, though. I was thinking I might need a bit of prayer to help me cope with Mum B's upcoming truth.

When it finally came in, however, it wasn't as bad as I had dreaded. It did make me laugh, though, because it's a truth a lot of mothers don't talk about.

To: Mum C
From: Mum B
Subject: Truth

C,

Recently, Mum A mentioned a 'don't waste water' speech she'd felt obliged to give to her daughter because other mums were listening. I'd like to know *your* true feelings about the environment. Are you a reluctant recycler, or do you rejoice in seeing how few litres of water you can use per day, opting instead for mother-spit as a cleaning product at every opportunity? Do you hate yourself every time you throw another box of Huggies in the shopping trolley, or do you secretly hug *yourself* knowing there won't be any tedious nappy pailing for you? Do you swelter through the summer, or flick the air-con on with gay abandon? Do you really give a shit about the environment, or do you think it is yet another way of keeping womankind busy and stuck at home?

I would love to hear your thoughts …

B

January

Forgive me, Mother Earth, for I have sinned. It's been ten days since my last confession. In these ten days, I have gone through two boxes of Aloe Vera infused tissues due to a wretched cold that attacked me somewhere between Brisbane and Sydney. And, Mother, it gets worse, for those tissues were 4-ply. I feel shame, but please take into account the five non-infused, 2-ply, cheap tissues I used. And please remember the rawness of my nose after using them. Be fair.

I am sure you will be pleased to hear that my son avoided the wretched, rainforest destroying cold. However, forgive him for he knows not what he does, for he avoided the cold and got the gastro. Two bulk packs of name-brand nappies and two bags of wipes later, our savings account holds the grand sum of $6.29, while the landfills hold everything else, smeared with poo. And while I used altogether far too many nappy sacks (oh, Mother, the smell! It has been burned into my very soul!), I must insist that some of those hail Al Gores should be handed to my son. After all, it was his fault. There's nothing that I have been feeding him that could cause such a profound stench, thus I am sure he's been sneaking in rotten eggs and cabbages when I haven't been watching. In that vein, please allot the penance for excessive water usage, as a result of the seven hundred million loads of washing, to him. Believe me, I did not want to deal with the aftermath of poo leakage. And if you could possibly see fit to remove that virus from the earth, it would be much appreciated. It isn't pleasant, you know. Not for anyone. Honestly, Mother, what were you thinking?

Aside from tissues, nappies, wipes, plastic bags that smell like talcum powder and an inordinate amount of water and detergent and fabric softener, we've been good. Really, we have.

Oh, wait. We went on holiday ... by plane. I know, I know, the fuel, our carbon footprints, the rape of our soils and all that. But I really do feel that I have paid for that sin already. Aside from the fact that our return flight was cancelled, we were left waiting at the airport for five and a half hours, *with a toddler*. Mother, we were punished. A lot.

So, tissues, nappies, wipes, plastic bags that smell like talcum powder, lots of water, detergent, fabric softener and plane fuel ... and real light bulbs.

Mother, be reasonable. Those fluoro eco greeny light bulbs are *awful*! They take forever to get to full brightness, leaving you in a wrist-slashingly depressing dimness, and when finally they reach full brightness, you feel like you're in an operating theatre. All that bright harsh light. No warmth. You half expect to look down and see a little, pink, loud person emerging from between your legs. Yes, Mother, I do know about the warmer toned bulbs but seriously, have you seen them? A glow worm breaking wind emits more light and joy.

Besides, when your Warrior came to fit those lights, she also took our shower head, cheerfully and piously claiming that we 'wouldn't notice any difference'. Well, Mother, we did. I once imagined that it was terribly romantic to bathe in tropical rain, the gentle drops washing the day from my body. Since obtaining that new shower head, I have seen that rain washes away nothing, it just leaves skid marks. It was a good idea in theory, I admit, but in practice, it really sucks. It really, really sucks. Strong water pressure is good. I used to be clean in less than five minutes. Now, I'm still in there 15 minutes later, trying to get the slickness of the conditioner out of my hair, all the while hoping that the silence from the living room means that the little rascal is still being entertained

January

by the gyrations of the Wiggles and not that he's taken my furniture apart.

And no, Mother, I will not become one of those people who doesn't wash their hair. I know you have tried to assure me that the greasepot, snow-flecked-shoulders look will only last a couple of months, but a couple of months is all it takes to acquire the manic look that sees everyone edge away from you on trains and buses.

Did you notice that, Mother? I still use trains and buses. Surely that counts for something? It proves that I try. Even though my shopping bulk has nearly doubled since the birth of my little boy, we still diligently carry our shopping back from the shops in those terribly chic green bags. We get to and from appointments at the hospital by inflicting eardrum piercing shrieks upon the general public as we sit in the stifling heat of a bus. Getting somewhere is a pilgrimage. We take food, drinks, books, annoying toys that get thrown out of the window and, when toilet training begins in earnest, a little Tupperware container that will be delegated to official public pee-catcher. And we do all this with minimal grumbling. That must count for something.

It just doesn't do to be blasé with the environment anymore. At every turn we have someone *Inconvenient Truth*-ing us, telling us what a dire state the world is in, terrifying us. And, while the big people continue to wreck the environment with their excess in everything, it is us little people that they proselytise to. 'Conserve electricity', they harp, all the while leaving the lights on in every building in the CBD all night. 'Conserve water', they say, while erecting yet another useless water feature. 'Use fuel efficient cars', they say and yet I haven't seen any of the politicians driving hybrid cars or, heaven forbid, catching a train to work. No, they sit in their homes and offices, lit with incandescent light bulbs inside and flood lights outside. They drive their fancy petrol guzzlers to and from every appointment. They give the go ahead for industries to wreck delicate environments. And I bet their showers have decent pressure, too.

We mums have the added guilt of those gorgeous little faces that we wake up to umpteen times a night. In those dark, small hours, it's hard to ignore the fact that the world is going to hell in a hand-basket, fuel is fast disappearing, the polar ice caps are melting, and the zinc mines are all but depleted. And there's little old me, sitting beside my adorable little boy, terrified of what the world will be like when he is my age. Will they have sorted out alternative fuel by then or will the governments, locked into more of their pointless bureaucratic arguing, have failed the people again? Will we have polluted the air to a stage where the world is in permanent smog like in those science fiction movies? Will our little corner of the world even be habitable with its soaring temperatures? Believe me, mummy guilt and green guilt combined is a quiveringly bad combination at 3am, while reaching for yet another Huggies.

So, Mother, stop targeting me. I get it, really I do. I buy fresh produce to minimise the amount of packaging I stuff into the bin. I separate my plastics, glass and paper, dutifully recycling everything that is recyclable. I wait until I have a full large load of washing before using the machine. I dry everything outside on the line, using the dryer only for emergencies. I buy wooden toys to save sending more broken bits of Fisher Price plastic to landfill. I have become the Drip Nazi, snapping at my husband if I detect even the slightest drip from a tap. I have even kicked him out of bed to go and tighten the shower taps because the pausing drips were driving me insane. It was like water torture with added green guilt.

But, please, let me wipe my nose in peace. And may I have my shower head back?

*

This truth haunts me in a way that the others didn't. Even admitting that I didn't want to be a mum and that I had, at one point, wished my son away, wasn't as bad as this. I get tense watching documentaries on the environment, terrified of what's happening in the world and what my son will have to grow up in. And the worst part is that I'm his mummy – I'm meant to be blessed with superpowers from the moment I start growing the placenta. I'm meant to be able to make all bad things go away.

But I can't.

I hate that I have these limitations, not for me but for him. It's terrifying. Sobering and terrifying. It would be easier for me to believe in a higher power, someone who is looking out for us, for the world, but I look around and see destruction, devastation, pain, famine ...

So I'm carrying on with my head in the sand as must most of the people in the world; hurting for my son, trying to shield him, trying to make a good life for him.

And on that note, I'm off to drown my sorrows with the others at our third meeting. It has been about five weeks since our last one and I could do with more than a few laughs. A good chuckle, combined with a couple of dirty martinis, a few more admissions of Mum B's even dirtier fantasies and I'm sure the world will look simply divine!

the third meeting

'Well, helllooo, anonymous ladies of the night ... or at least the late afternoon,' I said into the intercom in my best sultry voice and promptly buzzed Mum B and Mum C up to my hotel room for the second time and for our third meeting. On the fifth floor of the establishment this time, it took only seconds before the lift dinged, opened and they appeared in the hallway. 'This way,' I beckoned, holding the heavy door open for them.

'This is the same hotel, but weren't you on the other side of the hallway last time? And higher up?' Mum C looked around, confused, as the pair made their way towards me.

I nodded. 'I think it's done to confuse me. It's exactly the same inside, just reversed, and they seem to change me over from side to side each trip. I get up in the middle of the night and bash into walls. Once I almost peed in the walk-in-robe. I'm sure there's a camera somewhere and security are kicking back with a beer, laughing themselves sick.'

We were all standing in the doorway now. 'Should we air kiss?' Mum B asked. 'Or are we bigger and better than that?'

Mum C groaned. 'Apart from the fact that I'd need a step to reach up to Mum B's height to air kiss, I think when someone knows you're taking down the environment singlehandedly and your pet sisterhood hates, you don't need to air kiss anymore.'

'Probably true,' Mum B winced.

'Nice to know I'm still an enigma to you both,' I grinned. 'Come on in. Coffee, or alcohol?'

'I'm guessing Mum B needs a good, stiff drink,' Mum C replied, passing through the doorway.

'Make that two,' Mum B added, heading for the lounge room.

'I thought as much, so I got supplies this afternoon – gin, vodka, tonic, lime. And I ordered a sushi platter. It should arrive in about half an hour. I thought we could debrief then dehunger.'

'Sounds like a plan.' Mum B fell into one of the large armchairs, her bag dropping to the floor beside her. 'Now, if nobody asks me to move for quite some time, it'll be the perfect evening. It's been a long day and it started with water at breakfast. Okay, so my youngest wants water. I put water in a cup. A normal person would just drink the water, right? But then it's the wrong cup and then he wants ice cubes and then it's the wrong straw in the cup and the ice cubes are getting stuck on the bottom of the straw and he can't get the water up and ... I'm sure you've heard it all before.'

'Unfortunately, yes,' Mum C nodded. 'Most days. Don't worry, we'll just put our straws straight in the gin and vodka bottles and bypass that tricky ice altogether.'

We swiftly decided upon three gin and tonics and I cracked open a packet of chips. Within minutes we were all gracelessly reclined in one way or another in the lounge room. 'Now this is living.' Mum C held up her glass and the rest of us followed suit.

Before any awkward silence could befall us, I piped up, 'I have a little icebreaker for us. I was thinking it'd be good if we pooled our resources and skills on some critical topics.'

'Like?' Mum B glanced over at me. It looked like the movement actually took effort for the poor woman.

'Like on the important stuff.' I took a sip of my drink. 'I found myself doing some seriously sneaky work on a box of chocolates this week, which got me to thinking that we could start off today by telling each other the ways we've abused chocolate lately. For I'm sure you both have.'

Mum C nodded. 'Give me a second, for my answers may be many and varied.'

'Me too,' Mum B nodded. 'You start, Mum A. Tell us what you were doing with that box.'

I polished off another chip, dusted off my hands and got down to business. 'Okay, this week I opened up the bottom of a large box of Favourites, ate seven, re-glued the bottom with the skill of a forensic expert, and then took it to a family barbecue. Everyone was very surprised to find all the Crunchies and the Picnics gone. There was also a lot of comments about "settling" of contents.'

Mum C clapped her hands. 'That's good material. I never thought of the bottom of the box! All right then, I've got one for you. Earlier this week, I stashed the wrappers of a few fun-size chocolate bars in with a pooey nappy so no-one would notice them in the bin. I've also recently moved on to eating only Toblerone Fruit & Nut bars because of their excellent low hearability. Cadbury Fruit & Nut simply crinkles far too loudly. They really should look into that. It's a serious design flaw.'

'Good tip.' Mum B nodded. 'Though I'm afraid I haven't really pulled off any great feats of chocolate sneakiness this week. I've been doing a line in chocolate desperation – half a packet of chocolate melts hiding behind the salad dressing on the fridge door. It's not pretty. But that's what happens when you leave a girl treatless for too long. She'll eat pretty much anything.'

'So, the dare was pretty tough, huh?' I ask Mum B.

She sighed. 'Yes, and no. I liked the idea in a way, because I don't want to get to a place where I'm "needing" these things rather than just enjoying them. You don't want that once-in-a-while vodka and tonic treat sliding into alcoholism, you know?'

I nodded. 'I know someone who has the kids in bed at seven o'clock every night on the dot, and she and her husband then polish off two bottles of wine. And I mean that – every night. I sort of had her in mind when I thought of that dare. I wondered if she'd be able to do it. I think I could give up alcohol easily, but the treats ... I really don't know. Sometimes the thought of a chocolate bar after dinner is all that gets me through the long afternoon.'

Mum B shook her head. 'I'm clearly a lush because it was the alcohol that was harder for me. It's not just the drink, it's everything that goes with it – the quiet time with my husband, the knowledge that the kid part of the day is over. It's a personal thing, isn't it? Two bottles of wine is a lot, but I'm not going to judge her for it. Who knows? She may very well need two bottles after the day she's had.'

'Good to see you're sticking to being non-judgmental,' Mum C chipped in. 'I loved your truths about women. So true about the shoes. I've never understood the shoe thing.'

'I know!' I sat up a bit on hearing this. 'Honestly, those "shoes or outfit?" pieces in the magazines get me every time. Choose either the Jimmy Choos or the skirt, top, shoes, belt, necklace and bag? Yeah, um ... no contest there where I'm concerned.' I paused for a second, thinking. 'Though, oddly I do like to buy fancy shoes for my kids and ship them in from the US and Germany.' I turned to Mum C now. 'I guess that gives a new meaning to "carbon footprint", right?' I grinned.

Mum B laughed. 'You know, I tried those modern cloth nappies once. The researching and buying them was fun – cute colours and patterns, you know? The using them was not fun at all. How a six-month-old boy can pee out the back and sides of a nappy at the same time, I'll never know.'

'Oh, don't start on that,' Mum C groaned. 'The MCN crowd will hear you and then they'll start telling you the brands you should try – the all-in-ones, the inserts, the covers. You'll never hear the end of it! Modern cloth nappies are fab, really they are, if you have a big washing machine, lots of time and a large area in which to dry them. If it's raining, you're buggered.'

'I hear you,' I agreed. 'Some days the environment thing is simply another problem to add to your never-ending list, isn't it? When you've got two kids, a husband, two cats, a house and a job to run around after, the environment tends to fall by the wayside just because it's the only thing that won't whinge at you. Having said that, though, I do feel guilty when I can't be bothered to rinse out the peanut butter jar, I really do. Sometimes I've even gone back to fish the jar out of the bin at close to midnight because I've felt guilty about not doing it all day. But I have to admit, the Huggies are staying on my child's backside. They're the only bloody thing that works.'

'I'm sure our husbands worry about these things equally,' Mum C said solemnly.

The three of us cracked up at the mere suggestion of this.

'Maybe I could start a prayer circle about it,' Mum C continued. 'At least that would get my husband thinking.'

'Thinking about exorcising you, by the sound of it,' I laughed. 'I bet he's still checking the TV guide to see if you've highlighted anything slightly odd.'

'I really liked that dare,' Mum C mused. 'Though, it did end in a strange place. I honestly expected him just to rant and rave. But he didn't and then somehow we seemed to be talking about things again.'

'Again?' I questioned.

Mum C nodded. 'I think it helped us find common interests again that weren't focused on either our child or our future. We weren't talking about mortgages, home loans, where to live when uni. is over, or what the baby ate, said and learned today or how cute he looks in his Shrek ears. I think we'd been existing in each other's spaces without actually living with each other. Does that make sense?'

'Like roommates,' Mum B said and I nodded along with her as I took a sip of my drink. We both knew all too well what Mum C was talking about.

'Like roommates, but slightly worse, because we had to sleep in the same bed,' Mum C mused. 'There was an intimacy that was built a long time ago but we'd stopped propping it up. We were close because we were close, if you know what I mean. We weren't close because we knew each other.'

'People can become strangers in their relationships so easily, can't they?' Mum B agreed. 'You can see how it could happen. It's so easy to just stop working at it, to just reside in that comfort zone.'

Mum C inspected the chip she'd just picked up. 'Having a baby is the perfect way to fall into that. All of our energy was centred on him: where we'd birth, where he'd sleep, what to buy, what to do. When he came along, things were hard, so we only had the energy to deal with one other human being – the littlest one. When it became easier, we'd fallen into the habit of just plodding along, passing by each other, being comfortable but silent. It's good not to be silent anymore.'

'Your son is two now, right?' Mum B asked. 'Do you think your relationship is improving as he gets older?'

Mum C finished her chip before continuing. 'Slowly, but yes it is. I didn't think we were in dire need of relationship resuscitation but the dare showed me that even though things weren't bad, they could be better. And more than that, it gave me the chance to reconnect with myself. I like thinking about what my own opinions are on a matter.'

Mum B turned to me now. 'The affair dare was interesting.'

I'd been waiting for this. 'Painful would be a better choice of words,' I sighed. 'The weird thing was, when I started the dare, I wasn't even thinking about all of that – about Her. It just cropped up as I was writing …' I looked down into my drink for a second. 'But, quick! Let's talk about chocolate again.'

There was a pause.

'Still hurts, does it?' Mum B eventually asked.

I thought for a second or two, then shrugged. 'I never know how to feel about it, really. For him, it's something that didn't happen. For me, it's a very grey area. It's something that went further and he hasn't told me the whole truth; something that happened with more than one person; something that he thinks about when we're having sex. I don't know. So I try not to think about it and hope to God that he's not thinking about it as well.'

'He probably isn't, you know,' Mum C said quietly.

January

'You're probably right.' I shrugged again. 'But I'll never really know, will I? I guess at least I've now got the skills to vent about it, right?'

Mum B laughed. 'I loved the husband getting up at the last second and making coffee while you kept the world turning vent. I have so been there before.'

'Oh, good,' I said. 'I'm glad you liked it, because it's going to be part of my Big Dare.'

Silence.

Mum B bit her lip before continuing. 'I'm thinking this is where I should say, "What Big Dare?" in order to save myself from doing something completely life-changing like not jumping out of a plane.'

Mum C's eyes widened. 'I thought mentioning the "C" word at my house *was* the Big Dare. And that's "Christianity", not the other "C" word. As far as I'm concerned, things can only get easier after that. So, fill us in, what's your Big Dare about?'

I placed my drink back down on the coffee table. 'Well, I think writing down that one small coffee vent made me realise something – resentment is slowly, but surely, taking over my life. I heard someone a few years back say something that really stuck in my head and it went along the lines of, "Resentment is the biggest leg closer there is". It didn't mean much to me at the time, with just one child. But with two under my belt – wow. Resentment rules my world. Anyway, that's what I'm going to attempt to do for my Big Dare. I'm going to look at my resentment. Really grab it, take it apart and see what's making it tick. Because at the moment, I seem to be in this vicious cycle of doing more and more to make a point. Which is really not working out for me, because no-one bar me is noticing.'

'Ugh, I hate that,' Mum B said. 'I do that too from time to time. It never works. You just end up doing stupid things like cleaning the Venetian blinds really noisily all Sunday afternoon while muttering to yourself like a crazy woman.'

'Sounds about right,' I agreed. 'So, what about you guys?' I looked from Mum B to Mum C.

'I'm, um ... not telling,' Mum C finally answered.

'Me neither,' Mum B seconded.

I reached for the bowl of chips. 'I'll take that as, "I'm not telling due to my Big Dare's mind-blowing nature" rather than, "I have no bloody idea and haven't given it a moment's thought".'

'That's big of you,' Mum C laughed, lifting her drink up again. 'And quite true, though I'm not going to tell you which part you're right about.'

February

February

Mum A

I don't know about the other two anonymums, but my Big Dare was getting more and more interesting by the day. I was doing a lot of reading, and a lot of thinking. There was definitely more to this changing your life stuff than what I was eating for lunch and a half-hour coffee and newspaper swish. We do so much without questioning, forgetting that only a few things are really set in stone and that the rest is rather malleable. Now, I was questioning everything. So, after I'd read and thought, I read some more and took some notes and thought some more on top of that. It was sort of like a life sandwich. Hopefully it would turn out to be a yummy club-style one with fries on the side, and not that foul peanut butter job. I just had to keep working at it. Re-arranging it, adding to it. A glob of mayonnaise here, a pickle there …

To be truthful, things are actually going pretty well. It's just starting to head into the end of the slacking-off holiday season and the feeling of the real new year is creeping up (in case you don't know, the real new year actually starts after Australia Day). It's only after Australia Day and February approaches when I really start to think about what I want to accomplish in the next 365 days, other than not doing 365 grocery shops (high on my list). In the hope of checking my email less (I could hardly check it more), I've tried something new over the past two weeks – I've been working at the library and I'm getting a surprising amount done. So much so that I've realised just how much time I waste on things that give me less joy than completing a project (eBay, Facebook etc.). If I keep going to the library to write, I may even be able to achieve three-quarters of the writing I think I'm capable of this year.

As we're heading out of the old year (which was, I have to admit, one of the crappiest on record for my family) and I'm doing my Big Dare reading, and venting every so often about life in general to the other anonymums, I'm finding I'm actually a wee bit happier all around. It's as if I've opened the steam valve a little. Not turned it the whole way, mind you, just released a little pressure. Which is, I think, what I really needed to do.

While I'm crazily busy, spending each waking moment I'm not cooking something, washing something or wiping something up, writing my Big Dare, I find a few spare minutes to start to worry that this whole anonymums thing is almost over. Three Big Dares, a final meet-up and ... that's it. We're cured? Hardly. And I know it's a silly worry. We'll still all meet up whenever I'm in Sydney and I'll hardly regret losing the extra work on my plate. But I will miss the thrills: being told to sit on Santa's knee; letting loose my real thoughts; even exploring areas of my past I'd rather not think about. Perhaps we'll be able to challenge each other in different ways in the future (dessert eating contests, perhaps?).

I give myself another week of finishing my research, brooding and writing and editing before I realise, in the order of things, it's my turn to go first so I offer up my Big Dare. I cut and paste it into my secret email account and press 'send' with a very large gulp indeed ...

February

*

Having done the rounds of a lot of friends' houses as a teenage girl, I'd seen a lot of mothers in my time. And I'm going to have to tell the truth here and say that so many that I'd seen were bitching, whining, moaning nags. To be fair, two of them bitched, whined, moaned and nagged less, but this was probably only because they were preoccupied with the scotch they constantly held in one hand and the fag they constantly held in the other. At the time, I'd registered that what most of them said was true – they *were* put upon. Their husbands worked late and the kids were left entirely to them. And the kids weren't exactly grateful for their efforts. But the thing was, even at that young age, I realised all their bitching, whining, moaning and nagging, was all for nothing, because no-one was listening.

And then I had kids myself.

With my kids came the realisation that I now knew exactly what these mothers had been going on about. All the things they had complained about, I now had to do. Plus work, if I fancied doing that as well.

Pre-kids, things were actually pretty equal on the home front. My husband and I did the groceries together once or twice a week and tackled the housework on the weekends. Even with one child, a tiny two-bedroom apartment and two days of day-care, things were do-able. There wasn't too much shopping to do and not a whole lot of living space to clean. But then his job got more important. He took up some more study. We moved from the apartment into a house. We bought another car. We somehow acquired two cats. My job fell a little by the wayside in order to accommodate all of this.

And, slowly, day by day, my resentment started to build.

When I look back now, I can see that it started over the little things. The things he just didn't see. How could he not see he'd just left 5000 tiny freakin' hairs in the bathroom sink after shaving? How could he not smell that the kitty litter needed changing when he'd just been in the laundry? How could he open the bin and try to shove another two wet nappies in there when it was obvious it was full and needed emptying?

How could he?

I didn't know how he could, but I'd read approximately 5000 magazine articles in the past about men just not 'seeing' stuff (they didn't mention not 'smelling' stuff like the kitty litter, but I got the drift). Okay, I thought. I'll buy into the Mars/Venus crap. And I thought I'd get smart and fix these little irritations by designating specific tasks. You see, I stupidly thought that if my husband had specific tasks assigned to him, we would stop arguing about these petty, minor things. We discussed some of the tasks he could take ownership of, and one of the main ones that he decided upon was washing the bed linen and towels on the weekend.

Easy, yes?

Apparently not.

Because what all the lovely little 'quick fix' articles didn't cover was what you should do when he just doesn't step up and perform his allotted tasks.

What generally ended up happening was that around 5pm on a Saturday I'd take it upon myself to rip the sheets off the bed in a fury, having watched the minutes tick by all day while they remained, dirty, no ... *festering*, on the bed. 'I'm going to get to them,' he would say. Yes, but when? 5pm Sunday? In which case he'd take them off the bed, put them in the washing machine, add detergent, turn the machine on and that would be that. I would then be left to hang them out, get them off the line, fold them and put them away.

Not that I was keeping score or anything (and let's not even mention the towels ...).

The sheets and the towels thing drove me insane whatever happened. If he didn't do them, it would drive me insane. If he did do them and went to remake the bed (part of the deal), it would then drive me insane that a man with two degrees, entrusted with people's lives every day at work, could not manage to match seven items of fresh linen to go on a bed.

It sounds so very stupid, but it became a Very Big Deal. I don't think it was so much the sheets and the towels, but the fact that he'd agreed to do this one, simple thing around the house and then wouldn't follow through. And it was definitely *wouldn't*, because he could have done it if he wanted to, right?

Because I ended up doing his one chore, it became personal. He didn't care a damn for me because he *wouldn't* do this one simple task for *me*. The sheets and the towels symbolised what he felt about *me*.

Well, up yours, buddy, I'd think, ripping the sheets off at 8.15 on a Saturday morning. As time went on, I became so incensed, I'd rip them off while they were still warm – practically the moment he'd rolled out of bed. Stuff you, I'd think, as I stuffed them in the washing machine viciously.

As the years passed, this became my strategy towards many a thing, not just the sheets and the towels. *Oh, you can't do anything. Well, I'll do it, then. But I won't nag, oh no. I'll just quietly work on raising my blood pressure. Ulcer, anyone?*

I can't remember why we thought it was a good idea, but we had another child and moved into a bigger house.

I heard a saying the other day that went something along the lines of 'having one child is akin to having none'. How true that seemed to be the minute I had two. I'd managed to get quite a bit of work done with one child, but with two, I was struggling to meet the few deadlines I'd dared say yes to. My son was still tiny and I didn't want to put him in day-care, so I hired a nanny (no, that's too lofty a title, she was a babysitter, really) to play with him two half-days a week between breastfeeds. But she'd often text in sick, even though she was required for such a short space of time. Then there was the fact that my oldest wasn't exactly loving day-care and it hurt to drop her off there.

Work kept on going, and so did my husband. Each morning he gaily tripped out the door, not worrying about what we'd be doing (the miserable day-care drop-off for my oldest, or waiting for the babysitter's text) and forgetting the odd thing like his lunch or his mobile. I began to resent the fact that he could not worry and forget stuff. There was a part of me that knew this was ridiculous – that knew he had to work if we wanted to do frivolous things like eat and pay the electricity bills. But there was another, quickly multiplying, cancerous part that was taking over my brain and reminding me constantly that going out to work was his only concern – everything else just wasn't his problem. My work, family birthdays, medical appointments, sick kids, sick animals, sick cars, sick appliances, how the milk supply was faring today ... the list in my head went on and on and on and never stopped. They were the things I thought about last thing before I went to sleep and first thing when I woke up. I started to notice that when he asked about any of these things, I'd answer vaguely. Because he didn't really care, did he? And because he didn't really care, he also didn't deserve a proper answer.

Another year passed, bringing us up to just a few months ago. Several things had happened at once. We'd had to move house, again. We'd done this a lot in the past, but this time was a doozie, including finding a new rental in a tight market, organising repairs, painting a huge feature wall that we might have accidentally on purpose put a huge picture hook on and blah, blah, blah. All up, I lost about a month of work, which made me super-tetchy. We were also encountering a bit of stress on having to decide whether to hold our daughter back a year from starting school and doing the rounds of hearing tests, psychology appointments and the like in order to back this decision up. The days I spent running around after two different houses and medical appointments, and the nights I spent doing paperwork on two different houses, painting the feature wall, preliminary packing and whatever work I could possibly get in before midnight.

Thus, it wasn't really surprising when things came to a head.

My husband and I were due at a psychology parenting class at 7pm, right across the road from his work. I'd had the kids all day and covered arsenic hour alone, bathing the kids and making and feeding them dinner, then making us dinner. He'd left work at 6pm, got home, wolfed down the dinner, turned around and then, with me, drove back to his workplace. Neither of us was looking forward to the evening. We'd spent the last few weeks with experts telling us all the things that were wrong with our daughter and this was our last ditch $1500-group-therapy attempt to try and see if it would be at all possible for her to go to school in the right year. There were other, boring, problems as well. Now that our son was a little older, we'd long since ditched the babysitter and he was at day-care, but now his centre was closing and we needed to find somewhere new.

So, yes, to cut a long story short, things were already close to boiling point on the way to parenting class.

When we arrived in front of the building, there was one small parking space left, which would require a reverse park. Now, I'm not a terrible reverse parker, but I looked at that parking spot and just KNEW it would be the end of the evening's civilities. I had to take it, though. If I drove up the road and took another park, I'd be the incompetent wife, too ditzy to reverse park, and we'd be late. If I took the spot, I'd bugger it up. Not much of a choice, but at least I stood a chance if I had a crack at it.

My first attempt was pretty dismal, I'll admit. And at least my husband had the good grace to shut up during that one. The second attempt was a bit closer, but the directions started up from the passenger seat. 'Turn this way, turn that way. The front's FINE I SAID!' It was the third attempt that sent me over the edge. Because on the third attempt … he grabbed the wheel.

And that was it. Somehow, everything that had passed, or not passed, between us in the past few years, came to a head. And I didn't care that we were late, or that the car was sticking out into traffic. Or that the other parents going to the class were walking past. I sat there for a moment, then I let my resentment off its lead, turned around and said, steely-eyed, 'You know, I have been hating you for quite some time now.'

And then, that out, I promptly parked the car, and we went inside and played happy families for an hour and a half.

After I'd eyed off all the parents, wondering if they could see how I'd screwed my kid up as easily as I could see how they'd screwed up theirs, I spent the rest of the time wondering how my husband and I had become so miserable. How I'd gotten to the point of telling my husband I hated him. I don't think I really hated him, actually. I just hated our current situation. And it was easier to blame it on him than on anything or anyone else, like me.

We finally got out of the class and I told him I didn't really mean what I'd said. We both admitted we were pretty over things and we tried to talk about how we could change our current situation. We didn't come up with much and went back to the same old same old. Including me ripping the sheets off the bed and washing the towels during the week so he'd never get a chance to do them even if he wanted to.

Oh, God, it was pathetic how it burned me up, but I couldn't deny that it did. And what burned me up even more was that it was turning me into one of 'those' mothers. One of those mothers I'd seen growing up.

I decided I needed to sort myself out. Pronto. Before the transformation was complete.

I wasn't really sure where to start, so I started with trying to think about things logically. I realised that some things in my life were not going to change. A lot of the stuff I was seething about (packing kiddie lunches, doing load after load of washing, running around after everything and everyone) was stuff that I was simply going to have to do. This stuff was going to fall to me, because I was the one there to do it. Anyway, it wasn't like I really resented doing things like packing the kids' lunches or doing the washing. The kids had to eat and I was going to provide them with things to eat.

We needed to wash our clothes and I was going to wash them. I think the resentment lay in the fact that my husband didn't have that endless, monotonous list in his head all day, every day. The bottom line was my husband got to focus mostly on one thing: his chosen line of work.

The truth was I was straight out fucking envious that he got to do this.

Being a mother wasn't my forte. Is it anyone's? (If it is, and they're reading, they've probably long since thrown this book at the wall in disgust.) I loved my kids and wanted to bring them up well, but first and foremost, I identified as a person apart from them. As a writer. As me. My husband loved the kids as much as I did, but he got to be that other part of him every day. I didn't get to be that other, major part of me every day and it simply ate away at me. But that was the way it was going to be for the next three years, until the youngest hit school, and I had to come to grips with it before I got eaten alive.

So, when the anonymums started talking Big Dares, I knew this would be mine. I decided I wanted to change things. Properly. Not just in a 'you take the kids for a couple of hours on a Saturday afternoon so I can do something I want to do', but really change how our lives ran. Before it was too late and I was asking for a divorce as we reverse parked, rather than just telling him I hated him and had for some time (cringe).

My first thought was that I should book a session with a counsellor, but then I reconsidered. Maybe I should think about my life myself before I asked anyone else their opinion of it. So, where else to turn to? Where I always turn in times of trouble – books.

I went to a bookshop and scanned the self-help and

parenting sections. I didn't think the Dr Phil approach was really going to do it for me. It annoys me how his wife is always there, on the sidelines, gazing at him adoringly rather than doing something for herself. So I tried looking for different approaches. I ended up taking home four books:

Baby-proofing your Marriage by Stacie Cockrell, Cathy O'Neill and Julia Stone

The Post-baby Conversation by Alison Osborne

Buddhism for Mothers by Sarah Napthali

No Sex Please, We're Parents by Melanie Roberts-Fraser and Oliver Roberts

I read them in secret, one after the other, highlighter in hand. And here are my notes, detailing what I got out of each of them:

Baby-proofing your Marriage by Stacie Cockrell, Cathy O'Neill and Julia Stone

Plenty of good, realistic advice here. These are real women with real kids and real problems who want to provide concrete solutions to help with the everyday strife of life.

The little things I got out of it
- Perhaps think about looking at things from my husband's point of view. Would it be very nice to come in the front door each day and be immediately dumped upon with someone else's problems? I do this to him all the time, but I can't remember him ever doing it to me once. Geez, sometimes I even call him up to tell him how badly the day is going.
- I should show appreciation for the things he does do, not just resent the things he doesn't do (fair cop). I can see

how you'd feel like helping out more if what you already did was appreciated.
- Instead of getting cranky when he asks, 'What do we need to do today?' every Saturday (er ... the sheets and towels, perchance?), make a list of things that need to be done on the weekend (like the sheets and towels, dear) and put it somewhere visible.
- Get the babysitter in more often.
- Be intimate without having sex. I'm always scared that if I move towards him he thinks it's an instant invitation.

The big things I got out of it
- Have the right attitude. I need to change my attitude about many things from negative to positive, if possible, and if that's not possible, change it to at least neutral. If the kids are sick, it's more important that they are looked after and get better than I get my work done. My work always seems to get done eventually (sure, it gets done at 2am, but it gets done). Also, the sickness thing will happen now, while the kids are small, but will happen less as they get older. The stuff we're going through now isn't forever. It just feels like it.
- Blow jobs are fast and effective. They can buy you a couple of days and will leave him thinking he is more than a tad studly and irresistible (interesting advice, ladies! Certainly raised my eyebrows ...)
- Surrender. Yes, I'm lumped with a million things to do, which is a pain, but it's even more of a pain if I'm resentful as well. I need to look at things from a different angle. For example, if we're going to the park for the five millionth time, I can look at our trip as 'bleh, we're going to the park

for the five millionth time, my God, the tedium ...', or I can look at it as if I'm going to be spending the morning out of the house with my kids who, in just a few years, won't want to go anywhere with me at all. Another example from last week: if my husband is late home from work when he said he'd be finished at 6.30pm, I know it's for a reason. He hasn't stopped off at the pokies, he's dealing with an emergency. I know he can't just get up and leave at 6.25pm. I have to get a grip on this. He'll be home soon, and probably not much later than he said he would be. Odds are we'll all still be alive when he walks in the door (here's hoping).

- Make a list – what do I need in order to be happy? I need time to work. I need structured time with the kids. If I have a plan, neither I nor the children get as antsy. I need time to do the groceries without the tantrumy two-year-old, but the five-year-old is fine. I need time to exercise. I need time to go to the movies occasionally and a dinner out every so often.

Final thoughts
I can do this. Aside from my parents babysitting once a fortnight, I'll get the babysitter in once a fortnight as well. I'm going to ditch my attitude and not feel guilty about going to the gym or doing the groceries when the kids are in care. And I'm going to make a list of things we need to do on the weekend and stick it on the fridge. I am undecided on the blow jobs (have never been a big fan).

The Post-baby Conversation **by Alison Osborne**
There was so much I liked about this book, I hardly know where to start. It was just as if I was sitting down talking to my

beloved anonymums. It was refreshingly honest and simple, and there wasn't a single word of mothering bullshit. I only have a few points written down, which doesn't seem right, because I got so much from this book. It made me feel ... normal. It made me realise I'm not alone and that these issues that bother me so much on a daily basis are things most other mothers struggle with on a daily basis as well. I don't think I'd really acknowledged that.

The little things I got out of it
- Don't make requests with criticism and anger (oops ... maybe this is one of the reasons we have stalled on the sheets and towels thing).
- Identify the sources of conflict between you. What triggers emotional outbursts?
- Stop expecting and start requesting.

The big things I got out of it
- Have the sex talk. Bring the issue up and schedule a time to talk about it calmly. Acknowledge that my husband also has needs.

Huge realisation
- My husband is pretty hands on and will help me out if I ask nicely for things. I can't remember him ever saying no to a specific and fair request. He even says yes to the unfair ones! I think I might have scored a good one.

Final thoughts
Again, ditch the aggressive attitude. Ask nicely. Take a look at what sparks arguments between us. And see if we can

compromise on the sex thing (yes, believe it or not, we do argue about things other than sheets and towels).

Buddhism for Mothers by **Sarah Napthali**

Okay, I was sceptical when I bought this book. This Sarah Napthali – she didn't sound like my sort of mother. In her bio, it mentioned she was a 'former world traveller, former human rights activist, former corporate trainer, interpreter and technical writer' and a 'practising Buddhist'. I was more a 'former avid book reader, lounger and weekend sleeper-inner' and a 'practising chocoholic'. It sounded like she was the kind of gal who would think it frivolous if you paused to paint your toenails. But I decided to give *Buddhism for Mothers* a whirl because I could see how getting a little Zen with my resentment might work. When it comes to kids, the Zen-like mantra 'expect nothing' is probably more than fitting.

The little things I got out of it

- Be mindful of what I'm doing. Start with small 'being in the moment' tasks, like doing the dishes — feel the heat of the water, think about what I'm doing as I pick up the dish, rinse it, place it in the dishwasher, close the dishwasher, think only about the dishes. I can see how this might be very soothing and might help me to calm down overall.
- Even with the kids around, find one minute to concentrate on the rise and fall of my breath.
- Try yoga at the gym and incorporate a few moves into everyday life. If I find I'm having a lot of negative thoughts, try a yoga stretch or two to alleviate my funk.

- Make my thoughts transparent to my kids. If I get angry, take responsibility for it and tell them why I'm angry and what I could have done differently.
- When I'm peeved at my husband, turn things to the positive again. Remind myself of his good qualities. Sounds trite, but I do agree – often, negative thoughts snowball. Especially when you are reverse parking.
- Use distraction to change my moods. When I'm annoyed at my daughter for asking me to sticky-tape two dolls together for the 500th time (don't ask), instead of snapping at her, get up and tell her I'm going to catch and kiss her.
- Acknowledge what I'm feeling to help place space between me and that feeling of anger, anger, anger, frustration, frustration, frustration.

The big things
- Life isn't what happens when the kids are asleep, or in someone else's care (oh dear, that one hurt).
- Be present in the here and now and not mentally elsewhere. I can't enjoy my kids if I wish I was off getting other things done.
- I need to watch my ratio of praise to criticism. Just this morning I got into the car and called my husband on his mobile. He answered with 'Hello' and all I said was, 'Have you taken the garage remote out of my car?'
- Work out what really matters and what is mere bustle. So much of my life is mere bustle. I spent $150 on groceries yesterday, yet I found myself back there today spending $35 more. I am running around way too much, expending too much energy on doing things like picking up toys

(once in the evening is enough), dust-busting (once in the evening is enough) and changing the kids' clothes (it's okay to be a bit dirty, especially at home).

Final thoughts
Fine, so religion in general grates on me, but I really did enjoy the quick poo story the author included in this book and can see how a few facets of Buddhism could do me a lot of good. Being in the moment and being positive about the moment would not hurt at all. Calming my racing mind would be bliss. I've noticed that I have trouble having a nap when I get the chance, or sleeping further after I've been woken up in the early morning, because my mind races, thinking about all the other things I need to do. A bit of calm would be lovely.

And I really did enjoy that poo story.

No Sex Please, We're Parents by Melanie Roberts-Fraser and Oliver Roberts

I did stop to wonder if it was a tad odd to write a book about sex with your brother, but I'd argued enough about sex with my husband to give pretty much anything a go at this point.

The little things
- The relentless competition over who's done the most/has the harder life doesn't solve very much. I realised my husband was now too scared to say he was tired without first prefacing his statement with, 'I know you're more tired than I am, but ...'
- Be aware of flash points in your days (coming-home time, dragging Sunday afternoons etc.).

- Divvy up your time so you both get 'me' time – time together, time by yourself, time with friends, time with the kids.

The big things I got out of it
- It all gets better when they hit five. As they get older, you're more a family unit and it's less 'us and them'. Everyone's getting unbroken sleep, the kids are less needy and you'll probably feel more like having sex again.

Huge realisations
- It's okay to schedule time for sex. We plan everything else in our lives, so why not plan sex, too? I'm sure he would be happier with more sex that involved not having to beg me for it every time (am still considering the blow jobs …).
- I was really surprised to read a lot of men thought having sex once a week was a lot and that many couples were having sex once a month only and some far, far less than that. We were already close to around once a week. Maybe things weren't as bad as I initially thought?

Final thoughts
Quite a few good tips here. I really liked the idea of ditching the romantic notions about sex and scheduling it for times you're more likely to feel like it, which would mean an end to his having to beg until I cave and give in (which I know he hates). Mum B mentioned the scheduling thing as well during our last meeting and I'm intrigued that it's popped up again. There must be something to it.

No good poo story, but maybe I just have high expectations of all literature now.

February

*

It's only been a week since I finished my reading, but I've already started to make some of my changes. For a start, the list of things to do on the weekend has gone up on the fridge. I've let go of the notion of finding a new, 'perfect' day-care spot for my son and have now hired a 'real' nanny three days per week because I have a scary amount of work on. I'm trying not to feel guilty about it. I rationalised the decision by telling myself it works better for us (it solves our problems for care in the kindy holidays for our oldest). It also means we're not as sick all the time with day-care illnesses.

My husband and I made time to sit down together for a bit of a calm chat and have divvied up our weekends into four units – my husband sleeps in Saturday morning until 7.30am (sadly this is a sleep-in for us now) and I go to the gym around 8.30am while he takes the kids to the park. Saturday afternoon, he does something for himself (bike ride etc.) and I take the kids. Sunday morning I sleep in and then we have family time (go to the park/animal sanctuary/visit friends or family etc.). Sunday afternoon we either spend at home, go for a swim, or I pop out for a few groceries so I don't have to do that during work time. Both the evenings we spend at home, or get my parents to babysit, or get the babysitter in.

We also had the sex talk. As is often the case, his sex drive is higher than mine. It was interesting to be able to quiz him about sex without being in the moment of him asking for it. He said he'd have sex every day if he could, but he also admitted there were plenty of days when he was too tired, or was feeling a bit sick, or just wanted to watch TV or read. We also looked at how many times a week I'd be interested in having sex. My libido said about once every six months, but I knew this wasn't really true. I noticed if we didn't have sex for a fortnight or so, I started to miss not the sex, I think, but the intimacy of it. I ended up telling him I'd probably be looking at having sex once a week and we ended up compromising on twice ...

Mondays and Fridays (TMI?!).

We've only done one Monday so far, but I can see it working. He doesn't have to beg and I don't wonder if his hand will go a-creeping tonight.

This week, I've also tried to start looking at my husband differently. Not as someone who should be doing things for me, making things easier for me, but as a person with his own needs, inner thoughts, wants and dreams. Which is sort of how I used to see him, I guess. Back when life wasn't just about getting everyone through the day so we could move on to the next one.

And the sheets and the towels? Well, the towels I ignored and the sheets I took off the bed on Saturday, but he got the fresh linen out of the linen cupboard, matched it and put it on the bed.

And I said thanks.

Not five minutes later, when he asked me where the mop lives, I told him, ran into the next room, tried to recall my yoga postures, and ended up doing the good old downward dog.

Wish me luck and good contraception.

February

Mum B

I have to confess that the whole Big Dare thing really threw me. Every time Mum A asked about it, I fudged an answer and then was left thinking 'holy crap'. And then, one day, I realised that I was right in the middle of my Big Dare without realising it.

You may remember me mentioning that Husband B has a hankering for the rural life. He wants to chuck in our inner-city love nest for the wide open spaces of country living. I have been very unsure about it all – actually, downright terrified. I hate change. There, I've said it. Hate it. It's so uncool, but there it is.

I know we're supposed to embrace the new and the different, but I don't. I happen to be very comfortable where I am. In my ever-decreasing rut.

But all along, my Big Dare has been dangling in front of me. Without me even realising it, the other anonymums have been working on me to be more open to change, to taking the parachute jump, or making the seachange. Throw my life overboard, so to speak.

What does moving to a small town have in common with parachuting? Stepping into nothing, with no support, heart in mouth and a plummeting feeling somewhere in your stomach ... just for starters.

All along, my one rule for this game has been no parachutes. But that's what this Big Dare, this situation, entails. I know what the other anonymums would say – after everything we've talked about, what do I have to lose? I say plenty.

When Husband B first brought up this seachange malarkey, I laughed. I thought it was just one of those things that he'd get over. But he didn't. Every month, he got more and more serious about it. And then, crunch time was on us.

You may remember my week without alcohol and treats, and the family evening walk where he took advantage of my weakened condition and got me to agree to think about change.

Well, now he's done the research, found a prime location, even looked into schools, for heaven's sake. He's looked at job prospects, lifestyle factors and coastal properties. To sum up, he wants to go, now.

So my Big Dare is upon me. Can I, for once in my life, be brave enough to go 'what the hell?' without projecting 15 years into the future and seeing myself crocheting at the CWA (do they even do that anymore?); without wondering whether I'll be able to get a decent latte, or a dumpling, or a Pho – all staples of my comfy inner-city lifestyle.

I am not a leap-before-you-look girl. It takes me days, months, even years of soul-searching before I so much as change my fragrance.

Sometimes being sensible is good. Being able to point out the checks and balances in any situation. You say tomato, I say 'full of acid, lots of seeds, juice that stains white t-shirts'. You see?

But sometimes being a stick in the mud is bad for your love life. Always being the one to say 'but have you thought about ...' makes the other person think you're no fun anymore. I confess that I'm stubborn, and stuck.

February

Well, I'm under pressure to move. Like those cartoon characters whose feet come out of the quicksand with a 'whump!' sound, I'm being shoved from behind by Wile E Coyote brandishing ACME dynamite.

I'm not happy.

Day 2

Still not happy. I can't believe I can't come up with something else for my Big Dare. Something that would take the pressure off this decision. But it had to be big, and this is the biggest thing in my life right now.

Maybe I should have put my hand up for that Brazilian.

Day 7

A week has passed, a sleepless week. I have been thinking a lot about my reaction to all this talk about moving and have come to the conclusion that I am a complete wuss (you probably already knew that, but I'm slow). You'd think that Husband B was asking me to up sticks and move to Mozambique to live among the buffalo (if they even have them there). Do life choices really come down to latte choices? I can't believe what I've become. And I can't really blame motherhood for this. Well, maybe I can a bit.

I think that being a mum makes you cautious. Your eyes are suddenly open to every little harm that can befall your child, from spiders in their shoes to boiling saucepans on the stove. There's a tendency to want to live your life in a safe manner, a controlled manner. Sticking to the routine because you know how it turns out.

I don't know how this move would turn out – for me or the kids – and that scares me. Would we all be so miserable that Husband B and I divorce in a swirl of recrimination and arguments?

Alternatively, would we spend the rest of our lives feasting on chocolate paddle pops by the beach?

Anything could happen.

The other thing about being a mum is that you want to take the easiest route possible. It comes from spending those early days dragging the contents of your house with you every time you walk to the mailbox – nappies, check; wipes, check; three changes of clothes just in case, check; snacks for older child, check; water for older child, check; muslin wrap just in case, check; heavier wrap just in case, check. You know the drill. It got to the stage where simply never leaving the house became the best option. Or if I did go anywhere, it was to another safe house where I knew that wipes, juice, nappies, snacks and all the other rigmarole were available.

I just want an easier life. Moving the whole gang is not the easy route. Staying put and curling up into a ball, now that's easy.

Day 21

Well, we're going. I've been worn down. If it's not the broken record of my enthusiastic Husband B telling me how much I'll love it, it's the little digs from my cyber girlfriends. I stupidly told the anonymums my dilemma and they rallied, instantly infiltrating my Facebook page. I started getting status updates like this:

'Mum C is wondering if Mum B has packed her bags yet.'
'Mum A is thinking that Mum B is a big girly wuss.'
Childish? Yes. Effective? Definitely.

They're probably right. I've got nothing to lose. And if the truth be known, they're only saying what my inner voice is chanting. It's not really about them at all. They've graciously given me some leeway – my Big Dare will be allowed to be written in instalments and collated at a later stage.

I've agreed to try it for a year.

Six weeks later

I think the removalists removed my sanity. A word of advice: never try to organise a move for two adults, two kids and a goldfish (RIP Willy, who didn't last the trip) in six weeks. We have prised ourselves out of our former home, dumping about three truckloads of miscellaneous 'stuff' along the way.

I feel cleansed and purified and very Zen. Where did all the stuff come from? How did the four walls of our little cottage contain it all without bursting at the seams? Was our cottage actually a Tardis in disguise? That would explain why I feel like I've come through a time warp and landed in a much more spacious world than I'm used to.

It's very green here. Quiet too. And who the hell knew that there were more than four stars in the sky every night? Turns out that the lights from a city airport have enough power to obliterate an entire solar system from the sky. I have yet to venture too far from home. Instead I'm concentrating on putting things away. Everything looks different in a new environment. The kids are still running around in circles, but at least they don't look as though they're chasing their tails anymore – rather as though they've found a new orbit. We've decided to systematically try all seven cafés in town until we find the best coffee. It's good to have a purpose.

Week 1 (AS - After Seachange)

Speaking of ease of purpose, smaller towns are clearly designed for ease. All the services are provided within two blocks and it takes about 30 minutes to cover the bank, Medicare office, RTA, dropping off the photos to be printed, organising newspaper deliveries, buying the milk and bread, picking up a family assistance form, going to the post office and joining the library. Even with two kids in tow. Hot damn! I could get to like this.

Week 2 AS

The downside of getting everything done in five minutes a day is that you realise that there's nothing else to do. Our survey of the town's cafés has been cheering – we've covered three and would go back to at least one – but then it's a case of 'okey-dokey, now what?' No Supa-Centre in which to while away a few hours, pondering the relative virtues and energy ratings of new dishwashers that we cannot afford. No large mall in which to poke about, looking at clothes you'll never buy and distracting the kids on the climbing gym. What do people DO around here?

It makes you realise how much time we spend shopping.

When the hell did it become a legitimate pastime instead of a chore? Do we actually believe that dragging our kids to the shops is entertaining for them? I don't even enjoy shopping myself. But if we don't take them there where do we take them?

I've been checking out the local teenage population (purely for research, you understand, no Bill Henson overtones) and can see that if we stay here long enough, my boys will need to at least pretend to be surfie types. God, maybe they'll actually become surfie types.

At least I don't have girls. Paris Hilton is clearly the *muse du jour* in this neck of the woods.

Week 3 AS

We have a social life! Well, if one playdate constitutes a social life. When I first had Big Boy, I realised that I was going to have to reach back into my memory and find the skills that allowed me to make friends. Not work colleagues or drinking buddies, but friends. When you have to approach people cold-turkey, without the social lubricant of a glass of wine, in a playground, you realise that your skills base in this area might be, ahem, lacking.

Even so, back then I managed to end up with a great group of local mums. Some of them followed me home from the playground, having picked me up. For others, I got out my 'friendly face' and did the running. Starting with the desultory 'how old is yours?' chat and, in rare cases, moving directly to hysterical laughter about the business of being a mum. If I told a woman that I'd given the boys chocolate wafers for breakfast because that's all I had in the cupboard and she didn't laugh, she wasn't for me. The women who tried to one-up me with tales of bad motherhood, however, well now – talk about friends for life.

Why am I telling you this? Because I'm back at the park, wary, willing to be friendly but worried in case I attract that over-eager mum who wants to be my best friend from day one and drop her kids off for the afternoon on day three.

I'm also trying to avoid anyone who wants to play Baby Olympics and one-up me all morning with tales of her world-beating, gifted-and-talented one-year-old.

Please.

I tell you, it's a minefield out there.

But so far I've successfully negotiated it, even out-running the mum whose boys tried to beat the crap out of my two within the first five minutes while she looked on indulgently and said 'aw, they're getting on great'. Uh-huh.

But I did find one potential BFF. She's a woman about my age – no mean feat in a place where the average age for motherhood seems to be less than 21 (oh how I miss the older mum scene of the city) – who was trying to read the paper while feeding grapes to a baby and pushing an older child on the swing. My kind of girl.

We've tentatively arranged to meet at the duck pond next week. And then we'll see.

Week 4 AS

My new friend has turned out to be just not that into me. I arrived at the pond, dragging along two kids who didn't even really want to go to the park, bringing my best stories and self-deprecating one-liners and – nothing. She didn't turn up. I am officially rejected.

Remind me again why I came here? This bravery stuff is for the ducks.

Week 5 AS

Things are not going as well as I'd hoped. There, I've said it. When people talk about moving house being one of the most stressful things you can do, they forget to mention that it doesn't end once the removalist truck is unpacked and rumbles out of your life leaving you (and a sea of boxes) in your new home. I don't think my stress levels have been this high since the awful period in my life – and I do mean awful – when I had a bully for a boss. It was not knowing what each day would bring that did it then, and, frankly, now.

Husband B is settling in to his new job very well. He's already one of the boys, with Friday night drinks under his belt. Which just highlights my situation in stark, fluorescent (none of those energy-saving bulbs here) whiteness. I'm lonely. Despite having the constant company of my two little growths (whoops, children), I am starved for companionship.

When I try to talk to Husband B about it, he speaks in clichés about 'giving it time', about how things are 'darkest before the dawn', how there are 'plenty more fish in the sea'. I'm waiting for 'a stitch in time to save nine' and my collection will be complete. He's right – clichés don't become clichés for no reason. But you can't go for coffee with clichés either.

All I can say is thank God for the internet. I have become obsessed – to the point of probably requiring an intervention and rehab – with my email. Obsessed: I'm checking it every five minutes, minimum, and double-clicking 'check mail' just in case it missed something the first time around. I'm on Facebook every alternate five minutes, hungry for status updates and addictively updating mine. Just to prove I still exist, I think. I found myself writing this the other day:

Mum B is ... trying to think of something witty to write.

Five minutes later, I came up with this: Mum B is ... still thinking.

I did this, and I kid you not, every five minutes for two hours. Until my Facebook friends began posting comments that suggested they were concerned for my mental health. I desisted. I don't want anyone to think my brain has gone to mush because I've left the big smoke.

Even if it's true.

Week 6 AS

Today I met a guy who moved here 13 months ago. He told me it had taken him 12 months to settle in. Twelve months. That's a lot of worrying status updates.

Week 7 AS

She is into me! She just didn't have my mobile number with her to call me when her cat vomited all over her sofa, necessitating several hours of cleaning. My duck-pond friend was back at the park today, full of apologies, and wondering why she'd ever agreed to get her kids a cat.

I guess I have a friend. I definitely have a date – and

a number to confirm – for more fun and games with our feathered friends (and the kids) next week.

If I were watching someone else go through this, I'd be laughing, but the fact is that it's not that easy to make friends when you get older. And there's nothing worse than being stuck with someone for the sole reason that you have kids in common. All you talk about is the kids and I just don't think that's healthy – for you or the kids.

I'm watching Big Boy try to make new friends at pre-school and I think we're on about the same level. When you're under five, however, you can simply sidle up beside someone, start doing the same thing and then go home and tell your mum you have a friend. Not sure that works when you're old enough to have a mortgage.

Week 8 AS

I have become obsessed with the question of whether a small life can be a good life. To the point where I have begun interrogating people in the shops and banks about how long they've been in town, whether they've ever left, if not, why not, etc. Husband B caught me at it the other day and told me I sounded like a superior twat when I asked the bank manager whether he'd really never thought about trying something different. I guess I did, but it wasn't meant to be judgmental.

I'm truly interested. It occurred to me the other night over a glass – okay, several – of wine that the most content people in the world must surely be the ones who thought small. It's the moment that you believe you have to 'live large' that brings you undone. The minute that you seek out what you don't know. Stick with what you know and contentment shall be yours.

Or something.

I think this is one of the reasons that mums of our generation are so torn. If we'd been brought up to have kids and stay at home, sure, we'd have bad days but we'd be doing what we knew and chances are we'd be content. After all, we'd all be at home together, doing the same thing, so most likely there'd be someone in the same boat right next door. That's not the case today.

But we have been offered more. In fact, we have been offered it all. And now we tear ourselves into pieces trying to fulfil every part of our destiny. Our destiny is fractured, which means our contentment is fractured.

Am I suggesting we go back to the old days? Not for one minute.

But that doesn't mean they were all bad.

I'm beginning to think that I'm not having a seachange. I'm just finishing up the Me Change that began the minute I agreed to take part in this game.

Week 9 AS

If you'd asked me a few months ago whether I could see myself tap dancing, I'd have laughed; I am not a joiner. And yet, here I am, shopping for noisy shoes. It's all Husband B's fault.

He woke up on Monday and told me he'd had the best idea ever while he was sleeping. I should have stopped him right there. Given the amount of snoring going on during the night, there was no room for a good idea, let alone a 'best' one.

He'd decided that we should make Monday a 'yes' day. We had to say yes to anything that someone asked us that day. (I knew I should have kept him away from Jim Carrey movies ...) He was so enthusiastic, so thrilled with himself, that I said ... 'yes'. Forgetting that it was just that enthusiasm that had got me into my small-town mess in the first place.

So there we were. At first I thought he'd simply use it as an excuse to ask for sex every five minutes, but I underestimated him.

Instead, I found myself agreeing to tap classes. He told me that we were going to open the paper and join the first class that his finger landed on. It's his way of making me get out there and join.

I got my own back, though. I asked him to wash the dishes and vacuum the car when he gets home. There has to be something in it for me.

Week 10 AS

Brush, brush, stamp. Brush, brush, stamp. I'm sorry, no time to write right now, busy practising my new tap moves. With my little guys practising right alongside me. They are fascinated by my shiny new, very noisy shoes and exhort me to 'dance, Mummy, dance' every chance they get. It's hilarious and we are all having a wonderful time with it. Not only that, but the teacher assured me that tap is excellent for toning the legs. I could be cellulite-free for the first time since puberty, maybe. Perhaps this joining thing is not so bad after all. There were even beers after class. I could be a big fan of tap dancing.

Brush, brush, stamp.

Week 12 AS

The pictures are on the walls. You know you're staying a while when you've put hooks into the plaster. So this is home now. Still doesn't feel like home, but the longing for the little cottage in the city is beginning to fade. I'm now remembering how small it was, how there was no storage, how the boys bounced off walls that were too close together. The men in my life are settling in. They are making inroads into the community, drinking beers (the tallest one), deciding on favourite parks (the shortest ones) and making friends (all three). I think that as the sole female in the household, it's taking me longer, partly because I bear the brunt of worrying about the three of them. It's a woman's lot, is it not? Feed everyone else before you feed yourself. Worry about everyone else before you worry about yourself. Settle everyone else before you settle in yourself.

Am I sorry that I agreed to this? At the heart of things, no. I think that in the long run it will be better for all of us. I'm still missing peripheral things, though: cool bars, funky local restaurants, shops that don't send out weekly 20-per-cent-off-everything brochures. But the truth is that after the kids came along, I stopped spending a lot of time in any of those places. One thing about having kids when you are older is that you've had time to become tired of your extended youth. There are only so many binge-drinking sessions, ridiculously priced handbags and snooty meals a person requires.

So I've been forced to slow down, and that's not a bad thing. We spend more time together as a family now. I work from home, the kids are home, Husband B comes home. Time together is something a lot of people wish for – we have it, in spades.

My life changed. Surely that fulfils my Big Dare.

February

Mum C

Though I didn't tell the girls at our last meeting, I knew, sitting there with them, exactly what my Big Dare should be (definite emphasis on the 'should', there).

It certainly wasn't what I wanted it to be. I didn't want them to know, to egg me on, to make me do it. I wanted the leeway to be able to get out of it and indeed to pretend that this problem of mine simply did not exist, that it was a non-issue, nothing at all that needed to be dealt with. To say it out loud would be to admit that I wasn't normal, that I had some serious emotional hang-ups and that wasn't something I was ready to admit in public. Yet.

So I sat on it. I ruminated. I grinned as I read about their dares and saw that, although they were both quite scared of the decision they had made and the outcome from this, they both had a deep, quiet excitement behind the anxious exterior. Sure, Mum B was rebelling against a move away from the bright lights and big city (and probably, quite understandably, the availability of Pad Thai at 3am) but she was making a big move. New frontiers! Fresh air that didn't leave grey streaks on your face and a chance to see who you could be without the constant noise and stimulation of city life.

Mum A was taking control of her life, she was in the driver's seat and she would negotiate the road, reverse park and all!

It would be bumpy but she was determined and I imagined her wearing the manic grin of a *Top Gear* host. She was scared of where life had been going but she was changing that course, forever.

Fear and exhilaration radiated from them both and it made me so jealous. I wasn't at all excited about my dare. Not a tiny bit. It was fear all the way down to my toes and, because I knew how trivial it would seem to them, there was shame, too. Fear and shame made me shut myself away, locked behind my computer screen, safe from their demands, safe from their poking, prodding fingers. I thought that perhaps they would get sick of waiting for me to come up with a Big Dare and allocate me a parachute jump or something; an easy thing like that. But they didn't allocate me anything, just urged me onwards to find my own dare.

'Pssst! Mum C! Anyone there?' Mum B emailed.

'Are you lost in the wilderness of motherhood?' Mum A tweeted.

I cursed them for making me get a Brazilian earlier on – I could have done *that* for my Big Dare! Grasping at straws, I wondered whether I could trick my husband into getting the old 'back-crack-and-sack' and whether I could somehow spin that off as a Big Dare of my own. But time wasn't on my side.

'Where the bloody hell are ya?' This message came from both of them, via several different mediums.

It seems my computer wasn't nearly the barrier I had thought it to be and they could reach me. Message after message after message, there was no end. On forums, on email, on Twitter, on Facebook, even on my mobile phone through SMS. I couldn't avoid them any longer.

February

I knew what I had to do. I needed to run ... for my life.

This dare is hard. It doesn't sound hard on paper but it really is. It's difficult to get my head around it, mostly because my emotions and irrational fears are standing in the way, waving placards, hooting, jeering and yelling for attention, telling me all sorts of bad things will happen if I accept this dare. Not the run-of-the-mill silliness that might stop normal people, no, no, no. I don't fear having a heart attack halfway across the bridge. I don't think that I will take three steps and my feet will just suddenly fall off. My fears are never quite so devastating, they are far simpler, far less physically traumatic and far more insidious.

I'm scared, terrified, petrified, that people will laugh at me.

See Fatty run, they will quip, guffawing with their friends. Run Fatty-fat-fat! Wibble wobble! Fatty wibbble! Fatty wobble! Jelly on a plate!

In my imagination, the random jesters aren't terribly intelligent with their stabbing ridicule, but intelligence isn't the issue. It's the fact that they are thin and I am not, that makes them in my mind undeniably superior and better than me.

Let me explain ...

I am the sixth of seven children, and to anyone from a large family that should be explanation enough. Children are horrible little buggers. Not yours and mine, of course. Ours are absolute sweethearts with an angelic disposition, carved from the very essence of loveliness and tranquillity. But those other children, they are awful – deliberately and unashamedly cruel, pointing and hooting over everything from a stain on a shirt to a haircut. They travel in packs, hunting other children, tearing them down, destroying them. It's bad enough when they are at school but when they come home, they turn their aggression on the weakest, the most vulnerable poor sod who is outside the orbit of parental protection because the parents are too busy with the latest baby. In our household, that poor sod was me.

Being quieter than the rest of them and of the podgy disposition, I was the butt of all their jokes and all their jokes ran along the fatty-fat-fat line. Comic geniuses they certainly weren't but that never matters to the sensitive soul of a young child who is conditioned to trust her elders and does so when they tell her she is fat and that there ought to be a law against having bums that big. And no, you can't play, you aren't good enough. You're too fat to run. You be the goalie, you take up enough room for that.

And what did Fatty-fat-fat say in reply to all of this? Nothing, of course. Fatty-fat-fat went off to have another chocolate Hob Nob.

Growing up in the politically incorrect 80s, things were tough for the podgy kid. School uniforms weren't available in my size, for example. The horror of that stuck with me for years and the way my mother chastised me for being so fat still makes something inside me quiver. And you know what? I wasn't even that fat. I was a solid creature, with a bit of a belly, larger than average, granted, but not the obese heffalump I was being made out to be. But, coming home from the school uniform shop, dragging along my bag containing the skirt that was far too long for me but the only one able to wrap around my girth, being quietly and sharply told to be more like my skinny sister with every step we took, I felt like the single biggest thing in existence.

February

To make herself feel better, Fatty-fat-fat ate a Mars bar.

Being podgy in school was yet another source of unending torture. Remember the children that were horrible little buggers? Yeah, not only was I subjected to them at home but there was a fresh batch of them waiting for me at the school gate. Generally, I escaped the bullying that some of my fellow unfortunate chubs had to endure, but being picked last for sports, even though everyone knew I could knock a ball out of the court and kick a goal with better accuracy than any of the other girls, gave more food to the little voice inside that told me that I wasn't good enough, they were better.

Fatty-fat-fat fed her insecurities with a bag of salt and vinegar crisps.

I grew out of the puppy fat. My growth spurt hit and during my mid-teenage years, I was thrilled to be allowed to go shopping for myself and surprised by the ease with which I could find clothes to fit me in normal shops. I thought I was some monster that would have to go to large ladies' stores but no, I went to the stores my other teenage friends went to. Returning with a bag overflowing with clothes in a very respectable size 12, my mother sniffed and said that my sister used to wear size 8s and that she had to cinch in the waists of all her garments.

Fatty-fat-fat ate some Jaffa Cakes.

My weight has fluctuated all my life and, at my largest, I told myself I was a size 18 as I stretched the waistband of size 18 jeans to its absolute limit. I'm quite short, so the size 18–20 body made me look like a beach ball with legs. Toilet cubicles were too small for me to be in without feeling claustrophobic. I had to shop in special shops and if I walked into normal shops, shop assistants would come up and ask if I was looking to buy a gift. I would pick up garments and realise that they wouldn't cover one boob, let alone my entire top half. Walking for any extended period left me puffed and in pain, and I'd have to sit down. But the worst moment was when I turned up for work at a big name insurance firm as a temp receptionist. I had been temping for around six months and came to that office highly recommended, well qualified and eager. The supervisor, looked up, smiled and sent me off with the girl that I was to soon replace while she made a phone call. Moments later, I got a call from my temp agency and was told to go home because I wasn't what the company was looking for. I was back to feeling like that fat child, but this time it was real. I had real, undeniable outside confirmation that I just wasn't good enough, literally.

So, Fatty-fat-fat went home and demolished an entire pizza and a Fruit & Nut bar and a couple of cans of Diet Coke to cancel out the other calories consumed.

When I finally decided to lose the weight, I told no-one except my husband. I don't know what I expected people to say, but I knew I didn't want to hear it. I lost the weight quickly by going on a strict calorie-controlled diet, but refusing to exercise for fear of the potential teasing. When I decided to take the weight loss up a notch and did build up the gumption to join a gym, I made sure to work out only at quiet times and got desperately embarrassed if people looked at me because my face was red from the exertion. And while I sit here writing about it, I'm still feeling embarrassed. People aren't supposed to get all red and sweaty and disgusting from working out! Are they? Really? Why didn't the people around me look like that? Sure, they were red and sweaty but they didn't look disgusting ...

Eventually, I just stopped going. It was too embarrassing, too risky. People might laugh and my jeans were too tight to handle a Krispy Kreme binge. I haven't exercised in public since. Not even in front of my husband.

So, running in public, eh? It sounds so simple, easy, a nothing dare, doesn't it? I decided to do it ... tomorrow.

Tomorrow

I didn't do it. Wait, wait, calm down! I will do it! I just had too much on today to find the time. I know it's the permanent mummy problem, that our little ones are always somehow or other disrupting our plans, but this time it was a real reason. The little one was up all night with a rasping cough and decided that the only way to sleep was to do so with one knee on my groin, so that every cough would lend a painful jab, and an elbow to my throat to ensure that the same cough would cut off my air supply. He left one arm free to slap me across the face at various intervals whenever it looked like I might be thinking of going to sleep. Through the various and numerous tosses and turns during the night, I ended up with as much soreness as I would have had if I'd actually made it out for a run. Does that count? No? Drat.

After that night of no sleep, I had meetings, scholarship interviews, a couple of social engagements and a hot date with *House*.

The exhaustion is too much. And the boy is too sick and clingy. Will run under more amenable circumstances, tomorrow.

Tomorrow

Yeah, I didn't do it. But I have a good reason! No really, I do! Listen! My last foray into the workout world was to the gym many years and one child ago. I pulled out my running shoes and they don't fit properly anymore. Who knew motherhood could warp your feet? Anyway, having discovered the runners situation, I looked into the clothing situation. My track pants still fit okay. Not great, but well enough. The tops are fine. The jogging bras? Laughable. After the pregnancy and breastfeeding my son for two years, those bras simply could not cope with these deflated windsocks. These days I sneeze and nearly get a black eye.

If it helps to sate your sadistic side that was aching for tales of my pain and suffering, just remember that I had to go shoe shopping ... with a toddler. And if that wasn't hellish enough, I had to enter the torture chamber that is underwear fittings, where I was mauled and tutted at by a rejected officer of the Inquisition, my breasts inspected by disconcertingly red eyes, critically evaluated and rejected. All in a small, badly lit room ... with a toddler.

If I close my eyes, it's like I'm back there again. The screams, the prodding, the poking, the screams ...

Tomorrow

I didn't do it. And you're right, I am making excuses. Today's excuse was because I was too tired. I'm always tired. It's part of the job description when you're a mum. If I'm waiting for an energetic, rejuvenated day in order to go for this run, well, the phrase 'hell freezes over' springs to mind. So, tomorrow is the day. And this time, I mean it.

Tomorrow

I didn't do it.
   You're right. I do indeed completely and utterly suck.
   I tried to do it. I was all kitted out, new shoes, new impulse-buy track pants and t-shirt, floppy boobs tucked into new sturdy bra made from what felt like Kevlar and a bottle of pump pack water to complete the look. I walked down to Hyde Park, stood at the fountain and looked down the paths, wondering which one to take. I sat down on the edge of the fountain, feeling the tiny little misty splashes on the back of my neck.
   I couldn't do it. There were people around, laughing and pointing. Of course, not at me, but I had to look at them each time to make sure. Every chuckle, every squeal, every noise, I was convinced that it was all directed at me. My shame and fear made me completely self-absorbed, self-centred and egotistical. How utterly up-yourself do you have to be to think that everyone at a popular city park has got nothing better to do with their time than look at you? See, rationally, I knew I was being a complete and utter idiot. But my rational side was outnumbered and outmatched.
   I cheered myself on and tried to make myself get up and run a little bit, but I just couldn't do it. The childhood taunts filled my ears and I *just couldn't do it.*
   I walked back home, not stopping to indulge the voice urging me to buy a double chocolate thick shake.

After a bit of a sob behind locked bathroom doors, I devised a plan. The problem, I decided, was that I was going into this all gung-ho, no preliminary work, no foundations. So I'm putting that work in now. I picked up a couple of exercise and weight-loss books from the library and, while their approach to exercise is all very Nike-esque and 'just do it', I'm hoping it will provide the motivation to, you know ... just do it.

I've also started watching *The Biggest Loser*. I know that they are bigger and even more unfit than me. If they can do it, and do it in front of millions of people, so can I.

See how positive I sound? This is a new leaf, people! It's turning! Watch it turn! There it goes! Did you see it?

Give me four days and I'll make that run. You'll see.

Day 1

I'm perplexed by exercise and weight-loss books that have things like cupcakes on their covers. I pick up that book and think how I could just go a tasty sugary treat right about now. If I, someone who is not actually on a weight-loss diet at the moment (though I really should be) look at the cover and want to shovel some cake into my mouth, imagine what it's doing to the poor sods who are about to go into diet mode! There'll be a fair few people binging on cupcakes as a final hurrah!

Anyway, the exercise books aren't doing their thing and they simply do not work for me. They don't account for those of us who aren't scared of the physical distress but are terrified of the mocking, pitying looks of others. The motivations of 'you'll have more energy', 'release of endorphins', 'speeds up metabolism' read to me like 'blah', 'blah' and 'blah'. The books fall down because of one main fact: they assume that I am a rational person. Foolish, foolish books! Rationality around these here parts has been eaten like a snack-sized cupcake by the gaping mouth of fear.

The Biggest Loser, though, is actually working for me. They look uncomfortable and red and hot and sweaty, but when I'm looking at them, I think, 'Oh, cool! Look at her go!' not 'Fatty, fatty, wibble, wobble!' Is that because I'm not as cruel as other people? No, it's probably better for me and my current predicament to assume that people aren't generally cruel, otherwise I may never get this dare on the road.

Perhaps I need some inspirational music to play when I go running? Or perhaps music to play not to me, but to the general public. If nothing else, Shannon Noll at high volume would make everyone *else* run the hell away, right?

Day 2

I'm giving up on exercise and weight-loss books altogether and talking to a friend who is a personal trainer instead. I told her I was scared of running, but before I could complete my sentence, and in true hyper-energetic personal trainer style, she jumped in to tell me that I needed to stretch. All the pain from running comes from people failing to stretch properly, apparently. She got up, in the middle of the café in which we were sitting, and demonstrated the stretches that I ought to do before and after running. She then grabbed my feet to look at my runners (I'm wearing the runners all day every day to break them in properly). After this, she cast a critical eye over my bosoms and asked me to do a little shimmy so she could see whether there was enough support. I refused. It wasn't self-centredness making me believe that people were looking at us at that moment, they simply were. And they weren't looking, they were staring. Dragging her back down to her chair, I told her that my fears weren't really of pulled muscles or dislocated backs, or anything awful like that, but that I would look ridiculous and people might mock me. She told me that I should consider pilates and yoga. Puzzled, I asked her why. Would it give me more confidence? Make me look more graceful when I was running? Make me instantly tiny and gorgeous and never need to ever consider running? No, she said, she was recommending it for stretching, so there wouldn't be any pain.

It took a while, and many promises to be sure to stretch properly and frequently, to get through the Chardonnay fog that she had become mired in that afternoon and for her to finally realise that physical pain wasn't my worry. Her response to my actual problem was interesting. No-one will look, she assured me, because looking will make them feel bad. People feel bad about not exercising, so they tune out the people that do.

Well, well, well. What a revelation! I went from there straight to the park, sat down and watched people and it was true. Hardly anyone watched when joggers went past and certainly none of them commented. And, by a happy coincidence, one of the joggers was about my size!

Perhaps I will be invisible after all!

Day 3

Practice makes perfect.

I woke up today and was determined to run. Not the long

run through Hyde Park, that I'm terrified of, no, but there will be running. Definite running. I wore my runners with a pair of jeans, left the little one with his dad for a day of mess and mayhem and walked out, firmly closing the door on the excited shrieks and screams behind me. I wandered up the street, slowing as I approached the lights, waiting for the little man to go from green to blinking red so that I could run across the road. I saw a bus in the distance, so I ran to the bus stop to catch it. I ran up some stairs. I ran across the road when there wasn't a car coming. I ran a block, pretending to be in a hurry.

Incidental running. Running with purpose. Short bursts of energy. And no-one looked. No-one commented. No-one noticed. I had my ears pricked and listened hard. No-one was laughing. Maybe it was all in my head after all?

Day 4

Guess what? I did it. I really and truly did it.

I didn't walk to Hyde Park this time, so I didn't have the chance to get myself worked up into a mental frenzy before I got there. I started outside my building and at the first road, slowed for the green man, waited for the blinking red man and jogged across. I jogged up to the fountain, used the ledge for some quick stretching, all the time aware that there were people around and that I didn't look remotely like my gorgeous friend who worked out to earn her living. I ignored that inner dialogue, though; I very deliberately ignored the scared fat chick inside and looked down the path as if I was looking down the barrel of a loaded shotgun.

Now or never.

I had to decide who was going to win: me, the nearly 30-year-old mother, grown up, educated way past the point of her bullies and tormentors, happy and healthy (more or less); or Them, those shadowy creatures that lurk at the base of my subconscious, always niggling at me, always cutting me down, always telling me I can't do anything.

One foot went in front of the other, building up momentum. As I looked at the speed with which the third lamppost down the path was getting closer, I realised that I was doing it. I was running. And it actually felt good! Who would believe that it felt good to do this? Not me, that's for sure! I passed the lamppost and set myself a new target to run to, slowed to a fast walk as I started to get puffed and then sped back up if I thought my heart rate was dropping. Those exercise books had been good for something after all. Without realising it, I had internalised their teachings, was able to set myself achievable goals that were still challenging me by making it just that little bit hard. By concentrating on getting to the lamppost, the tree, the bin, the tent, I was not concentrating on who was watching me. I couldn't hear what anyone was saying, anyway; too much blood was rushing through my ears.

After a few minutes, I stopped, too puffed to continue, and looked around. The fountain was in the distance, sparkling in the morning sun. The hum of traffic was muted under the shrieks and laughter of children running around being chased by their parents. Young couples still in that rosy-cheeked phase of romance were lounging on the grass, talking in gentle hushed tones. They weren't looking. No-one was looking.

I carried on, determined that I would run a lap of the park. I passed another jogger who didn't even glance at me, focused instead on the direction from which I had come. No time to consider what he was thinking, I pressed on. And I realised that I wasn't thinking about him because I had other things to think about (come on, flowerbed, get closer) and he probably felt exactly the same.

It took a while to get the whole way around the park but the fact that I could do it at all, in my ridiculously unfit state, made me feel really good. And beating the living bejesus out of the Them in my head was completely priceless. I did it. I really did it! My feet were sore but stuff that ... I won!

I limped home after the run and spent the day feeling proud of myself. Sadly, I didn't feel energetic like the exercise books had claimed I would. Instead, I felt utterly buggered and didn't want to do anything much at all. What I felt overwhelmingly, however, was emotionally lighter. Like I could do anything. I even toyed with the idea of going for another run the following day.

But that didn't happen.

The aches and pains I'd inflicted upon my body for daring to take it out of its comfort zone were bad enough, but really, the problem was all in the toes. I had blisters the size of China on my little toes, so bad that my husband refused to even look at my feet for the next few days and, when he caught an eyeful by accident, would suck in his breath like he'd been punched in the guts. I couldn't put on socks, never mind shoes.

I haven't been running again since then. It's been three weeks and, though the blisters are long healed, there have been plenty of excuses not to: have work to do, can't find anyone to watch the little one, too tired, have a headache, too sore, want to sleep ...

So, no. I haven't been running.

But at least I now know I could if I wanted to.

I don't speak to my family very often for reasons that may be told another day, but after completing the Big Dare and getting out from under that sibling weight, I wrote to my sister. I did the usual email dance, telling her about my son, the hilarious antics he's been up to, asked about her and her job, asked after her children and husband, and then just threw in, 'I went for a run through Hyde Park today'. I wondered if she'd even notice.

The next day, I got a short email from her, which said, 'Good. About time you did something about it.'

I guess the reason for my not speaking to my family often doesn't need much of an explanation after all. Whereas a few short months ago I would have been a crumbled emotional mess, a Cadbury's Flake of a person, after confronting all I needed to confront and dealing with all that needed to be dealt with, I looked at the email, rolled my eyes and flicked it the finger before deleting it.

Fatty-fat-fat doesn't eat here anymore.

Feeling good about myself, my blistered toes bearing the battle scars of my new warrior state, feeling better for not allowing siblings to taint my victory, I'm looking forward to seeing the anonymums again. I wonder if it was enough of a dare for them? I wonder if they are too normal to get it?

February

the final meeting

I waited, hidden by a thick, marble-like pole until I saw both of them meet up. I held my breath as they said their hellos and then I counted down: three, two, one and then ran – my arms and legs flailing – all the way across Martin Place.

In the few seconds it took to reach them, people didn't just look. They pointed me out to other people so they could look, too.

Mum B and Mum C waited, watching, until I'd caught my breath before Mum B asked, 'What in the hell was that, Mum A?'

'That was people actually looking at someone running,' I laughed now. 'After reading your Big Dare, Mum C, I remembered that episode of *Friends*. The one where Phoebe runs like a lion's chasing her and Rachel's too embarrassed to be seen with her until she has a crack at it herself and finds out it's actually fun to run like a lion's chasing you. I went back and watched it again after your Big Dare and it's exactly like both you and Phoebe thought: "You don't care if people are staring, because it's just for a second and then you're gone!".'

Mum C and Mum B looked around. 'Actually, they're still looking,' Mum C told me.

I checked. She was right. A few were still staring. But I didn't care and shrugged. 'So, those ones we'll sell tickets to.'

'There's going to be a repeat performance?' Mum B smirked.

I looked at the 20 metres or so we needed to walk to get to our destination. 'If you run with me to the Lindt café, it's my shout.'

Mum C laughed. 'Now there's something worth running for.'

*

We perched on our high, caramel-coloured chairs and waited, drooling, for our chocolate feast. This place was like being inside a chocolate box. My tastebuds already liked it very much and I hadn't even eaten anything yet.

'Is it wrong to use skim milk in a hot chocolate that comes with a side of a large jug of melted Lindt chocolate?' Mum B pondered.

'You've got to cut back somewhere,' Mum C told her. 'It may as well be on the milk.'

'I'm guessing you're going to tell her she can start her diet ... tomorrow,' I teased.

'Diets, running, toilet training ... all things like that are better if you start them tomorrow,' Mum C grinned back.

'So, how goes country life?' I asked Mum B now, leaning forward to rest my arms before me on the long bench. 'Have you still got your friend and her vomiting cat?'

Mum B nodded. 'We've met up again a few times. I like her. We're different. She thinks my constant search for the best caffeine hit in the district is hilarious – she's just as happy with

Nescafé – but we can laugh at our differences. And that's taken the pressure off Husband B, too. He's not my main source of entertainment now.'

'Do you think you'll fit in by that 12-month mark the guy was telling you about?' Mum C asked her.

'I think so,' Mum B continued. 'I've realised that it's quite nice. Slowing down a bit, I mean. There's no shame in it. I'm not sure why I thought there was, really. I guess I was just one of those city people who couldn't understand why anyone would live without all that city stuff.'

'I bet the parking's dreamy.' If there was one thing I hated about Sydney, it was the traffic. Not to mention the parking.

'It is. I've only had to reverse park the car twice since I moved. Besides, I pretty much walk everywhere, so as long as that one café keeps up its crema standards, we'll probably stay.'

'Who would've thought it?' I raised my eyebrows. 'You! In the country! Pho girl!'

'Just don't ask me to move,' Mum C shuddered. Mum C was originally from London. She thought anything more than five streets away from the Sydney CBD was the sticks.

There was then a moment's silence as our plates were placed before us. A strawberry macaroon, a serve of chocolate cake and a hot chocolate. We breathed in collectively.

'Ooooohhhhh ...' we breathed out again.

'I told you it was a more than valid choice.' Mum B pointed out her hot chocolate to me. 'I told you it was substantial.'

Mum C and I nodded now. We'd thought she was piking on us by ordering just a hot chocolate, but that hot chocolate was a good two or three cups worth of liquid bliss.

'I'll never doubt your ordering again,' I told her.

'Does strawberry technically count?' Mum C eyed off my macaroon.

I lifted one up to take a nibble, then groaned. 'Yes. Strawberry counts.'

Mum C sighed as she looked at her chocolate cake. 'I could just stand up and slap this straight onto my thigh.'

I looked at her plate and then up to meet her eyes. 'Quit it with the guilt. Just eat it. And then go running ...'

'Tomorrow!' we all three said in unison.

*

'So, can we ask you about your resentment now that you're sated with sugar?' Mum B leaned back in her chair. 'Dear God, my stomach is actually making sloshing noises.' She wiggled around to demonstrate. 'Anyway, resentment?'

I licked the last of the macaroon crumbs off my fingers before I answered. 'Good, I think. You know, I'd say more than half of it was just acknowledging the resentment was there. That it existed.'

Mum B nodded. 'I get that. It's like the monsters in my youngest's cupboard. I find that if I just get him to say goodnight to the monsters in the cupboard, he's fine with them being there. It's weird, but it seems to work a whole lot better than trying to tell him they're not there at all.'

'I get where he's coming from,' I agreed. 'It's easier to deal with something you know is real. I needed to wrench my resentment out of the cupboard and things are a lot better for it, I think.'

'And the linen cupboard?' Mum C piped up. 'The sheets and the towels?'

I laughed a martyred laugh. 'What do you think?'

'That you're probably still doing them most of the time?' Mum B shot me a look that said she'd been there. And then some.

'Of course. But at least as I stuff them in the washing machine, I remember to turn around and tell him the kitty litter stinks and he needs to change it. There are worse jobs, and I'm giving them all to him.'

'Nice,' Mum C nodded. 'I guess that's all of us, then. Truthed. Dared. Big Dared.'

There was a pause as we looked at our empty plates and cups.

'So ...'

'Well ...'

'Um ...'

We were all thinking it. Our three months were up. What next?

'Have we found ourselves yet?' Mum C asked the question first.

We stared at each other this time.

'I guess the fact that we're here says something,' Mum B said.

'A lot, really,' I added. 'I mean, we could have given up at any point.'

'Or at the first wax strip.' Mum C's eyes widened slightly in pained remembrance.

'I almost never even got started,' I said, also remembering something – my reluctance to sit on Santa's knee.

'And I'm surprised I can even look you both in the eye, knowing what you know about me ...' Mum B shivered slightly. 'Is it cold in here?'

'Need something French to warm you up?' Mum C grinned.

'I'm going to ignore that,' Mum B said darkly. 'How about a proposal, then: we meet back here in a year?'

'A *year*!' Both Mum C and I sat up at the same time, rather shocked.

'That's too long!' Mum C added.

'Way too long!' I continued her theme. 'I need a good excuse to order garish cocktails that include crème de menthe on their list of ingredients. I like crème de menthe and there aren't many people I can drink it in front of who'll still talk to me. Apparently crème de menthe is très uncool.'

'Okay,' Mum B nodded. 'Since we have crème de menthe needs, how about meeting in another three months' time? You're right. After all, who else can I tell that my kids ate chocolate wafers for breakfast again?'

Mum C and I both breathed sighs of relief now. 'Three months is good,' Mum C told her.

'Three months is just about right,' I agreed. 'Three months should keep us on track.'

'To where?' Mum B asked.

We looked at each other again and I think we all realised at the same time that we didn't know. We didn't know where we were going.

But at least we now knew there was no shame in an uncharted destination. As long as we remembered to pause for a laugh about it now and again, we'd probably make it to wherever we were going. Maybe even with something of our old selves left intact.

Hopefully.

www.ingramcontent.com/pod-product-compliance
Lightning Source LLC
Chambersburg PA
CBHW032337300426
44109CB00041B/1087